grades **PreK–K**

SPRING/SUMMER

Thematic Literacy Units to Build and Strengthen

- **Phonemic Awareness**
- **Phonological Awareness**
- **Phonics**
- **Alphabet Skills**

and Other Early Literacy Skills

Managing Editor: Cindy K. Daoust

Editorial Team: Becky S. Andrews, Kimberley Bruck, Karen P. Shelton, Diane Badden, Thad H. McLaurin, Sharon Murphy, Kimberly Brugger-Murphy, Gerri Primak, Allison E. Ward, Karen A. Brudnak, Sarah Hamblet, Hope Rodgers, Dorothy C. McKinney, Janet Boyce, Beth Marquardt

Production Team: Lisa K. Pitts, Pam Crane, Rebecca Saunders, Jennifer Tipton Cappoen, Chris Curry, Sarah Foreman, Theresa Lewis Goode, Ivy L. Koonce, Clint Moore, Greg D. Rieves, Barry Slate, Donna K. Teal, Zane Williard, Tazmen Carlisle, Irene Harvley-Felder, Amy Kirtley-Hill, Kristy Parton, Cathy Edwards Simrell, Lynette Dickerson, Mark Rainey, Karen Brewer Grossman

www.themailbox.com

Table of Contents

K Is for *Kite!* 4

R Is for *Rain!* 14

J Is for *Jelly Bean!* 24

D Is for *Duck!* 34

M Is for *Mother!* 44

N Is for *Nest!* 54

F Is for *Farm!* 64

B Is for *Beach!* 74

G Is for *Garden!* 84

S Is for *Sunflower!* 94

W Is for *Watermelon!* 104

©2005 The Mailbox®
All rights reserved.
ISBN# 1-56234-620-2

Except as provided for herein, no part of this publication may be reproduced or transmitted in any form or by any means, electronic or mechanical, including photocopying, recording, or storing in any information storage and retrieval system or electronic online bulletin board, without prior written permission from The Education Center, Inc. Permission is given to the original purchaser to reproduce patterns and reproducibles for individual classroom use only and not for resale or distribution. Reproduction for an entire school or school system is prohibited. Please direct written inquiries to The Education Center, Inc., P.O. Box 9753, Greensboro, NC 27429-0753. The Education Center®, *The Mailbox*®, the mailbox/post/grass logo, and The Mailbox Book Company® are registered trademarks of The Education Center, Inc. All other brand or product names are trademarks or registered trademarks of their respective companies.

Manufactured in the United States
10 9 8 7 6 5 4 3 2 1

How to Use

1. Select a topic.
2. Choose ideas to enhance your lesson plans.
3. Use the reproducibles to strengthen skills and save you time.

Quickly assemble the literacy booklets.

Provide for practice.

Adapt the open pages to match students' abilities and skills.

 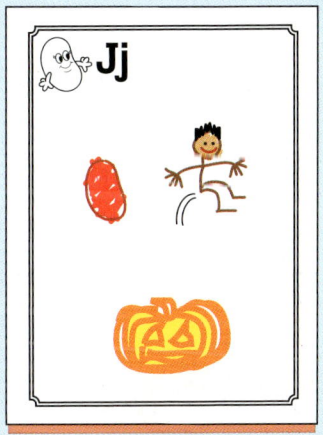 

Letter Recognition

Sound Association

Letter-Sound Association

K Is for Kite!

"Krazy" for Kites
Recognizing initial sound /k/

This class activity makes recognizing words that begin with /k/ a breeze! Give each youngster a construction paper kite cutout and five construction paper bow cutouts (see the patterns on page 8) along with a length of crepe paper. Next, have each student glue one end of the crepe paper to the back of her kite.

Gather little ones in a circle and have them place their kites and bows in front of them. Say a familiar word. Direct each child to place a bow on the kite's tail if the word begins with /k/, like *kite*. Instruct her to sit quietly if the word does not start with /k/. Continue in this manner until you have named five words that begin with /k/. Then have youngsters glue their bows to their kites' tails. If desired, encourage little ones to point to each bow while naming a different word that begins with /k/.

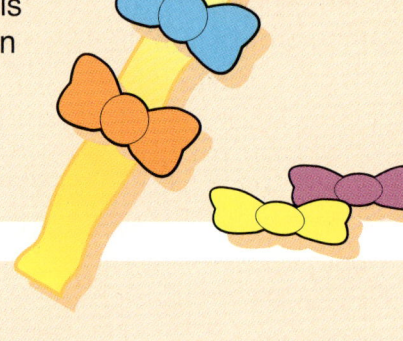

K-I-T-E, Kite!
Recognizing letters in words

Singing this song while using a kite pointer is a great way for youngsters to practice recognizing letters in a left-to-right sequence! Give each child a straw, a copy of the kite word strip on page 9, and a construction paper cutout of a small kite (pattern on page 9). To make a kite pointer, help each youngster tape his kite to the end of a straw. Next, teach little ones the following song. Then sing the song again while youngsters use their pointers and word strip to track each letter in *kite*.

(sung to the tune of "Bingo")

Flying kites is so much fun.
It is best in wind and sun!
K-I-T-E, kite!
K-I-T-E, kite!
K-I-T-E, kite!
Let's go fly a kite today!

Bring your kite; I'll bring mine too.
Yours is purple; mine is blue.
K-I-T-E, kite!
K-I-T-E, kite!
K-I-T-E, kite!
Let's go fly a kite today!

Send the kites up in the air;
They fly high without a care.
K-I-T-E, kite!
K-I-T-E, kite!
K-I-T-E, kite!
Let's go fly a kite today!

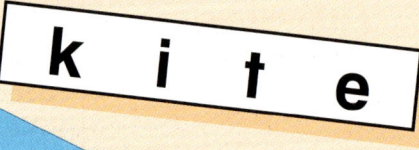

Kite Lotto
Making letter-sound associations

Give students' letter-sound skills a lift while playing this version of lotto! Write each of the following letters on separate small cards and place them in a paper bag: *B, F, G, K, L, M, R, S, T,* and *V.* Copy the large kite pattern on page 8 and draw lines through the center as shown. Then give each student a copy of the prepared kite and four different picture cards from page 10. To make a lotto board, have each youngster glue one picture card to each section of the kite. Give each child four game markers.

To begin, remove a card from the bag and announce the letter. Have each youngster identify the letter's sound and then attempt to match the sound with a picture on his board. If he has a matching picture, instruct him to cover the picture with a marker. Continue in this manner until one child correctly covers each picture with a marker. Encourage little ones to trade boards for another round of play!

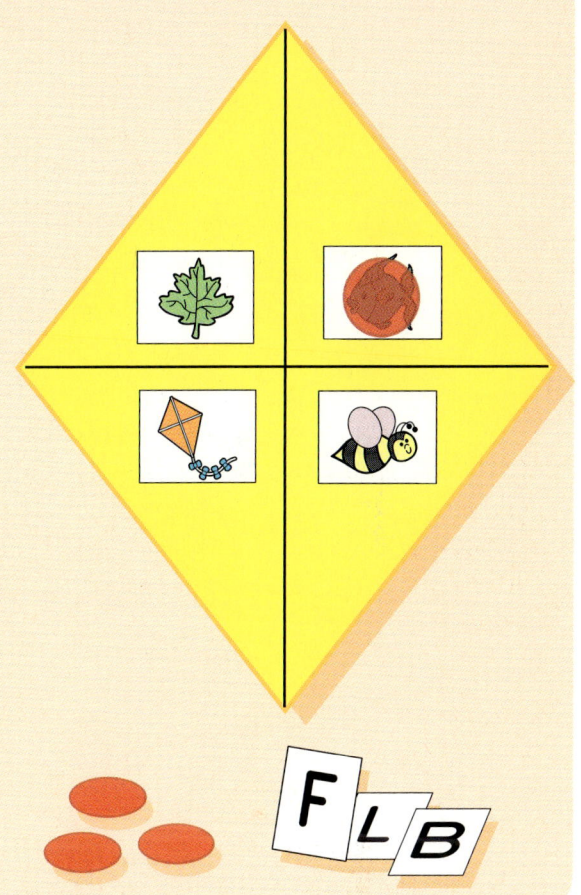

Out-of-Sight Kites
Following oral directions

This cool kite project provides a great opportunity for little ones to follow oral directions. Make a copy of the large kite pattern on page 8 and draw lines through the center as shown. Then give each child a copy of the programmed kite. Help each youngster identify the top left section of his kite. Give a direction for how to decorate that section, such as "Draw purple stripes" or "Draw yellow dots." Provide time for decorating. Continue giving directions for the remaining three kite sections. If desired, invite little ones to add tails to their kites.

High-Flying Sort
Sorting rhymes

Rhyming is a breeze at this center! Make a copy of the rhyming cards on page 10. Choose two sets of the rhyming pictures and cut out the corresponding columns. Set the remaining cards aside. Color the pictures and cut out the cards. Make two different-colored copies of the large kite pattern on page 8; then cut them out. Tape a length of crepe paper to each kite and place the kites at a center along with the rhyming cards. When a youngster visits the center, she sorts each picture card by its rhyme onto one of the kites. For additional rhyming practice, color and cut out the unused rhyming cards for little ones to sort.

A Brand-New Kite
Increasing print awareness, early writing

Take students' understanding of print concepts to new heights with this picture-perfect project! In advance, take a photograph of each youngster posed as if he is holding a kite string. Give each child a copy of the small kite pattern and the poem on page 9. Have him color the kite and cut it out. Working with one child at a time, read the poem and help the child write his dictated response on the blank line. Then assist each youngster in taping the poem, kite, and string to the photo as shown. Invite little ones to share their poems with the class. Display these high-flying projects for all to see!

I flew my brand-new kite one day.
It went so very high.
It flew all the way to ___Florida___
As it sailed off into the sky!

Soaring Around
Demonstrating an understanding of positional words

Kites and youngsters are sure to fly up, down, and all around during this class activity! Give each child a construction paper kite cutout and one bow cutout (patterns on page 8). Have each student glue his kite and bow to a jumbo craft stick. Next, direct him to glue a length of crepe paper to the back of the kite.

To begin, direct little ones to hold their kites and stand. Give a positional direction, such as "Fly your kite under the table" or "Fly your kite next to your chair." Instruct youngsters to follow the direction and fly their kites at the correct position. Continue in this manner for other positional directions.

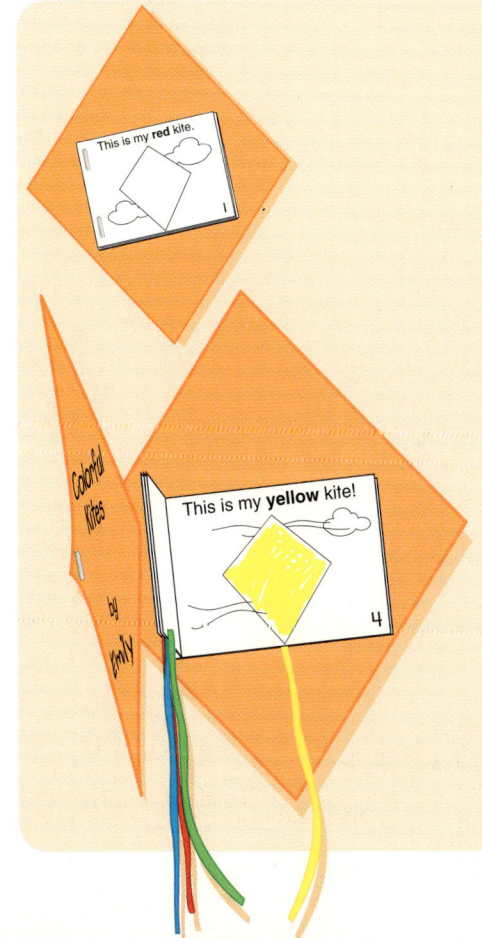

Colorful Kites
Recognizing color words

Your students' knowledge of color words is sure to soar when they make these kite booklets! In advance, obtain a supply of ribbon in each of the following colors: red, blue, green, and yellow. Make a copy of the large kite pattern on page 8 and label it with the title "Colorful Kites." Then make a construction paper copy of the programmed kite (cover) along with a blank construction paper copy of the kite for each student. Next, copy and cut out the booklet pages on page 11 for each child. To assemble the booklet, staple the sequenced pages atop the blank kite cutout. Give each youngster a booklet and read aloud each page as students follow along. During a second reading, have each youngster color each kite on pages 1 through 4 the corresponding color. Direct her to color a design on the kite on page 5. Next, help her tape a corresponding color of ribbon to the back of each kite on pages 1 through 4 and a desired color of ribbon to page 5. Staple the cover to the booklet. Invite little ones to read their booklets with a partner and then take them home to share with their families.

Large Kite Pattern
Use with "'Krazy' for Kites" on page 4, "Kite Lotto" and "Out-of-Sight Kites" on page 5, "High-Flying Sort" on page 6, and "Soaring Around" and "Colorful Kites" on page 7.

Bow Patterns
Use with "'Krazy' for Kites" on page 4 and "Soaring Around" on page 7.

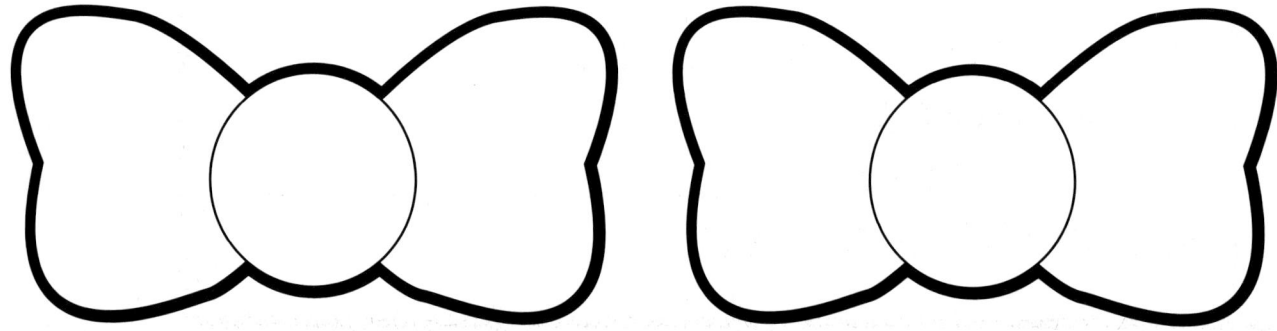

Small Kite Patterns
Use with "K-I-T-E, Kite!" on page 4 and "A Brand-New Kite" on page 6.

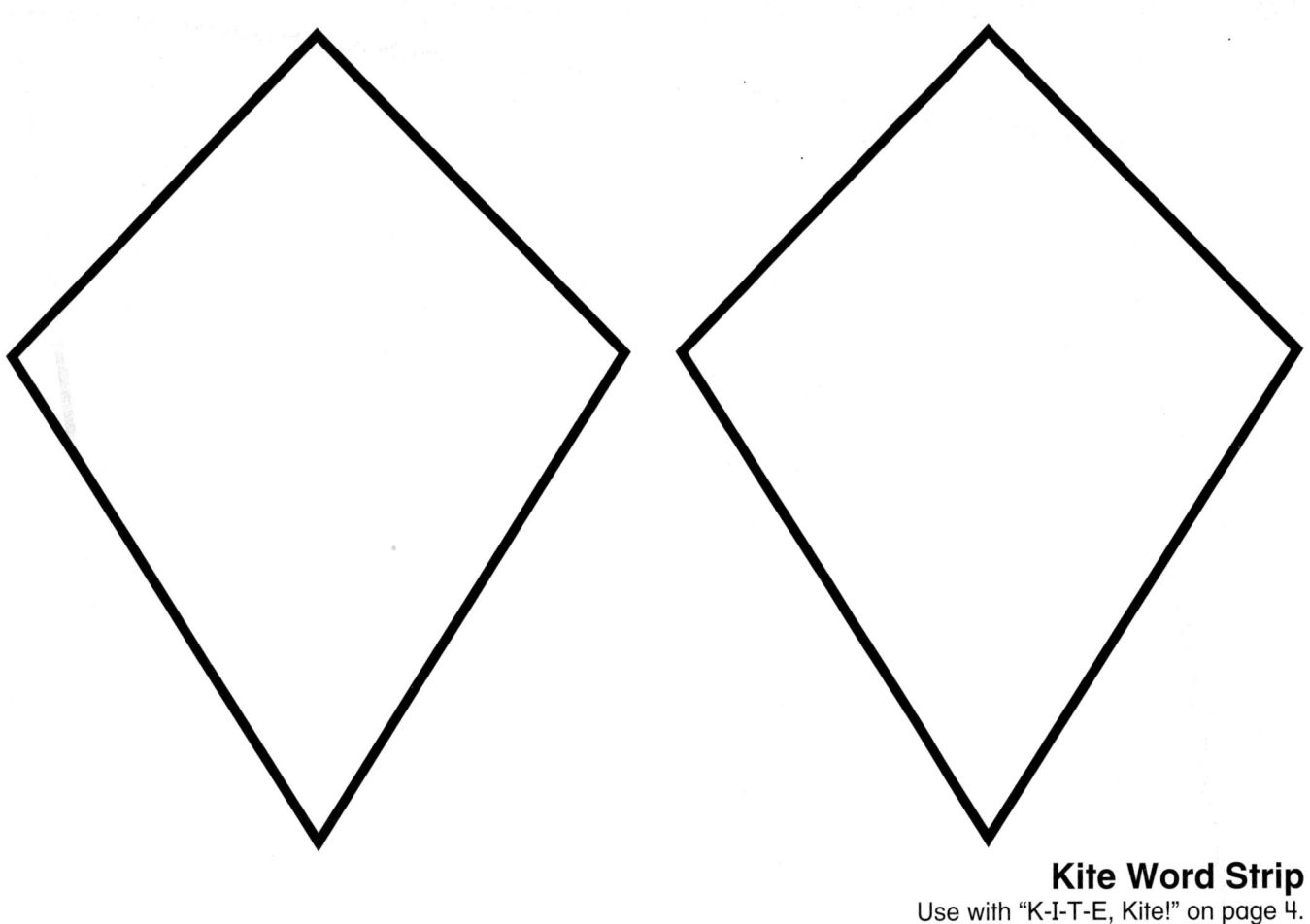

Kite Word Strip
Use with "K-I-T-E, Kite!" on page 4.

k i t e

Poem
Use with "A Brand-New Kite" on page 6.

I flew my brand-new kite one day.
It went so very high.
It flew all the way to _____
As it sailed off into the sky!

Picture Cards
Use with "Kite Lotto" on page 5.

Rhyming Cards
Use with "High-Flying Sort" on page 6.

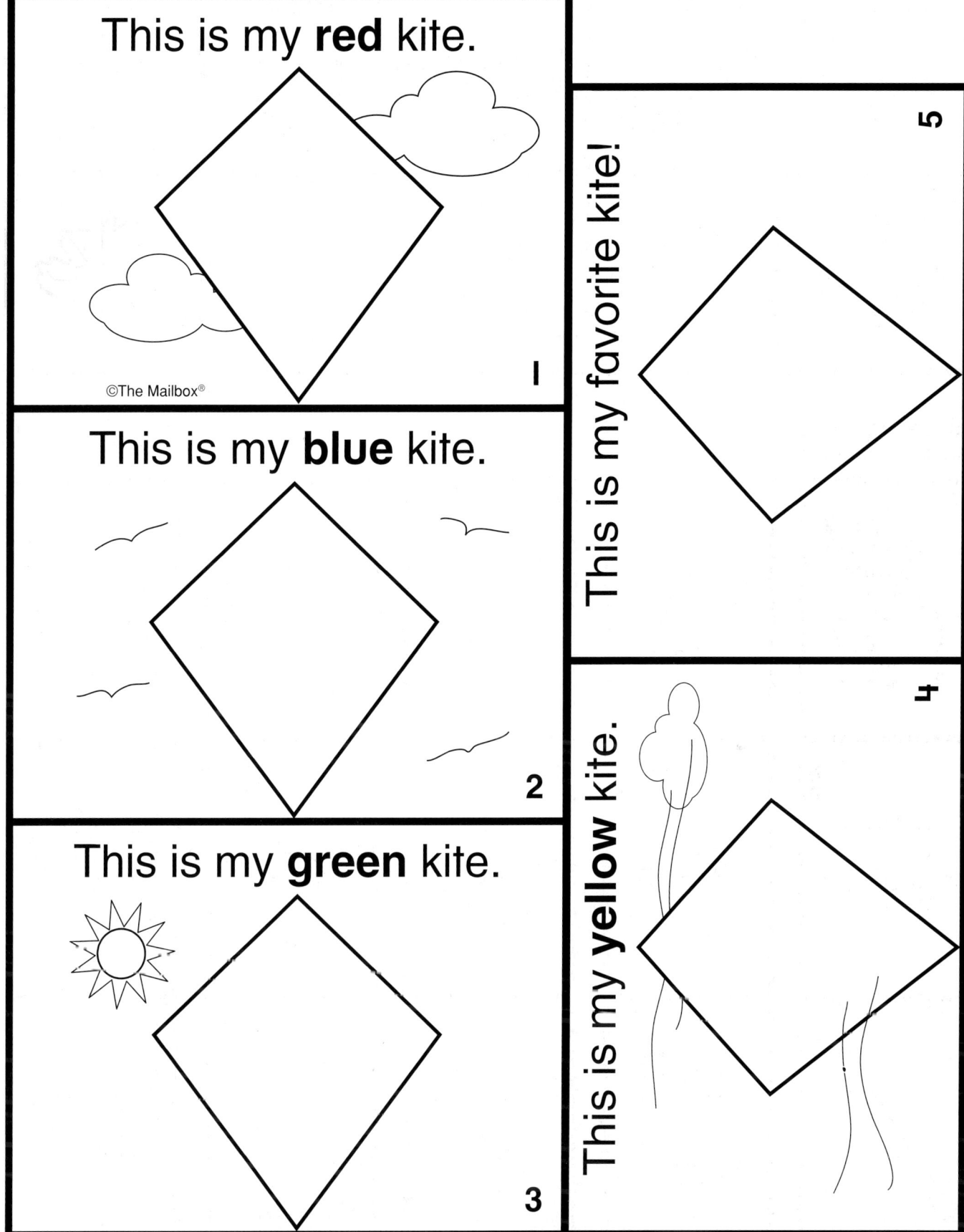

Name_____   Initial Sound /k/

Kangaroo's Kites

Color the pictures that begin with K.

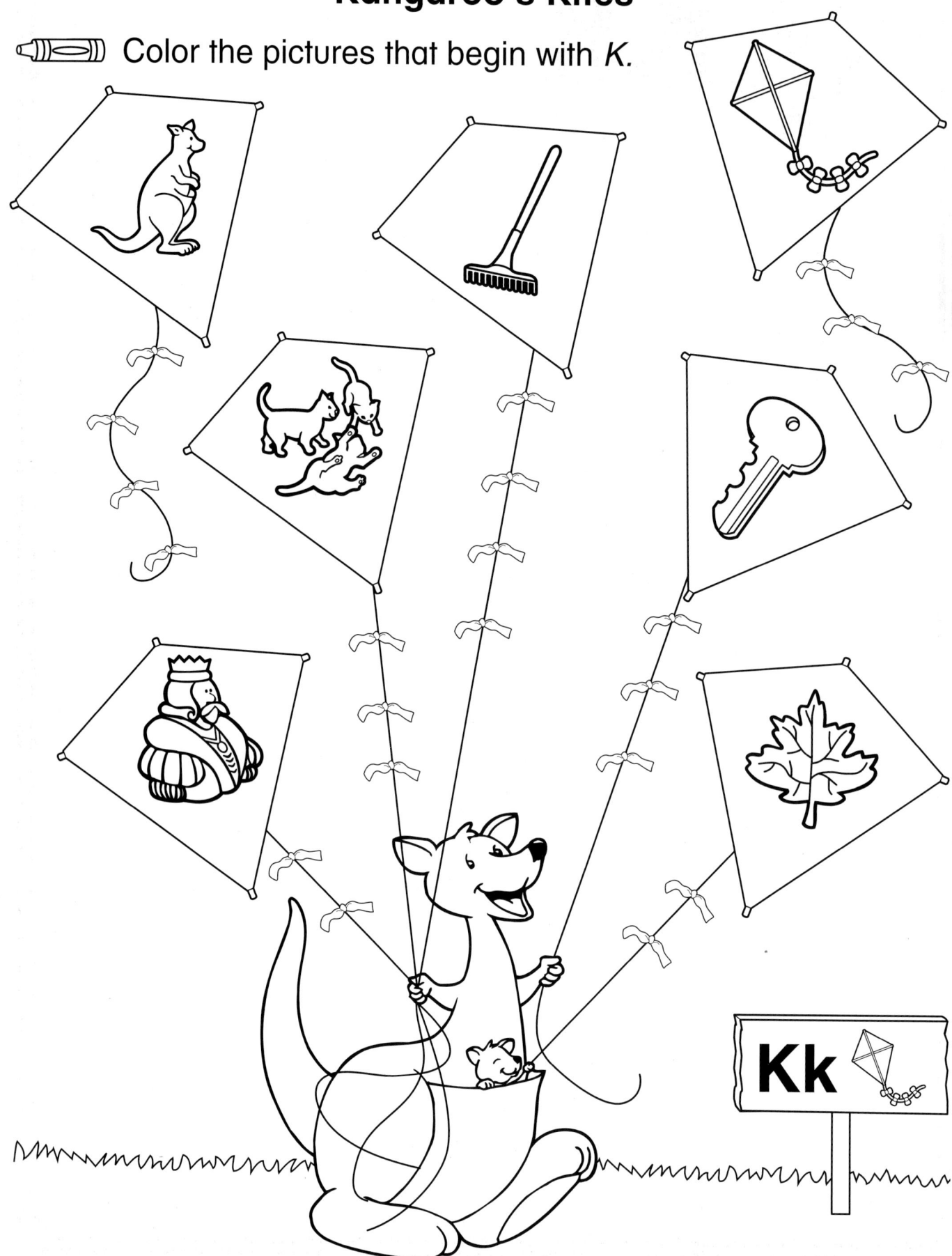

R Is for Rain!

Puddle Jumping
Recognizing initial sound /r/

Youngsters jump into sound-awareness skills with this gross-motor game. Take youngsters outside and have each child use chalk to draw a rain puddle on a paved surface. Next, ask each child to stand beside her puddle. Tell her to listen for words that begin with the /r/ sound, like *rain*. Next, say a word aloud that begins with /r/ and ask each youngster to jump into her puddle. Then have each student jump outside her puddle. Say other words, some that begin with /r/ and some that do not, and ask youngsters to jump in and out of their puddles for each /r/ word. Ready…jump!

Rain Shakers
Segmenting words into syllables

Shake up word skills with this fun activity! For each child, partially fill a film canister with rice and then secure each lid with tape. Also make a class set of the strip on page 18. Have each youngster personalize her strip and then help her cut it out. Wrap the strip around the shaker and secure it with tape. Say the word *raindrop* and have each student shake her rain shaker for each word part. Confirm that *raindrop* has two word parts. Ask her to listen and then shake her rain shaker to show the word parts for *rain*. After verifying that it has one word part, say the two words again as each child shakes her shaker for each syllable. Then announce additional words for students to repeat the activity.

Picture a Rainy Day
Recognizing initial sound /r/

Dip into sound-recognition practice with this rainy day game. Color a copy of the picture cards on page 19 and cut the cards apart. Place an open umbrella on the floor and spread the cards around it. Ask a small group of students to sit in a circle around the umbrella. Have one child choose a card, name the picture, and decide whether the word begins with the /r/ sound. If it does begin with /r/, he drops the card into the umbrella. If it does not begin with /r/, he drops it in a discard puddle. Students take turns repeating the process until all the cards have been chosen.

Rain Puddle Treat
Associating R with /r/

Splash into letter-sound knowledge with this fun snack. Give each child two mini rice cakes and a craft stick. Spread blue-tinted frosting on each rice cake to make a puddle. Ask youngsters to say, "R, /r/, rain." Guide each child to use the craft stick to write an uppercase *R* on one puddle and a lowercase *R* on the other puddle. Next, ask him to name the beginning letter and sound in *rain*. Reward each child by sprinkling blue cake sprinkles on each puddle. Then invite him to enjoy his tasty rain puddle.

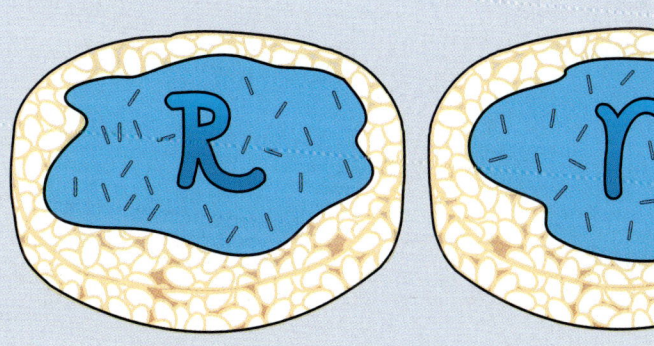

Ready for Raindrops
Identifying the letter R

Shower youngsters with beginning-sound practice! Copy the raindrop patterns on page 18 to make a supply. Program each raindrop with a lowercase *R*; then cut out each one. Gather students and have them listen for the /r/ sound as you say the word *rain*. Then ask youngsters to name other words that begin with the /r/ sound. Write each word in large print on a chart. Next, give one child a raindrop with rolled tape on the back and have her stand next to the chart. Ask her to identify a letter *R* in one word by placing the raindrop over it as shown. Repeat the activity with additional student volunteers.

raindrop
run
red
rabbit
radio
rose
race

Who Needs Rain?
Identifying the letter R

Little ones will absorb letter identification skills and learn about the importance of rain as they make this raindrop-shaped booklet. Copy pages 20 and 21 for each child and gather a stamp pad with washable blue ink. Read the text on each raindrop to students and discuss with them the importance of rain for all living things. Next, help each child make fingerprint raindrops on each of her booklet pages. Have her draw a self-portrait on booklet page 3 and then color each booklet page. Then help her write her name on the cover and cut out each page. Sequence the booklet pages with the cover on top and staple them behind the cover. Help each child read her booklet, and have her circle all the *R*s in each sentence.

16

Rain Cloud Writing
Writing the letter R

Youngsters burst with excitement as they practice writing skills with this fingerpaint activity. For each child, place a spoonful each of white and black washable paint onto the center of fingerpaint paper. Invite the child to mix the paint together to make a gray rain cloud. Then guide him to use a craft stick to write an uppercase and a lowercase letter *R* in his cloud. After the paint dries, cut out the clouds and display them on a bulletin board.

Letter Cloudburst
Identifying uppercase and lowercase letters

Sprinkle alphabet skills all around at this sorting center. To prepare, cut out one large and one small cloud from quilt batting. Label a set of raindrop cutouts (pattern on page 18) with uppercase and lowercase letters. Store the raindrops in a plastic pail and place the pail at a center. A child sorts the uppercase letters onto the large cloud and sorts the lowercase letters onto the small cloud. When finished, he picks up each cloud and sprinkles the raindrops back into the pail.

Raindrop Strips
Use with "Rain Shakers" on page 14.

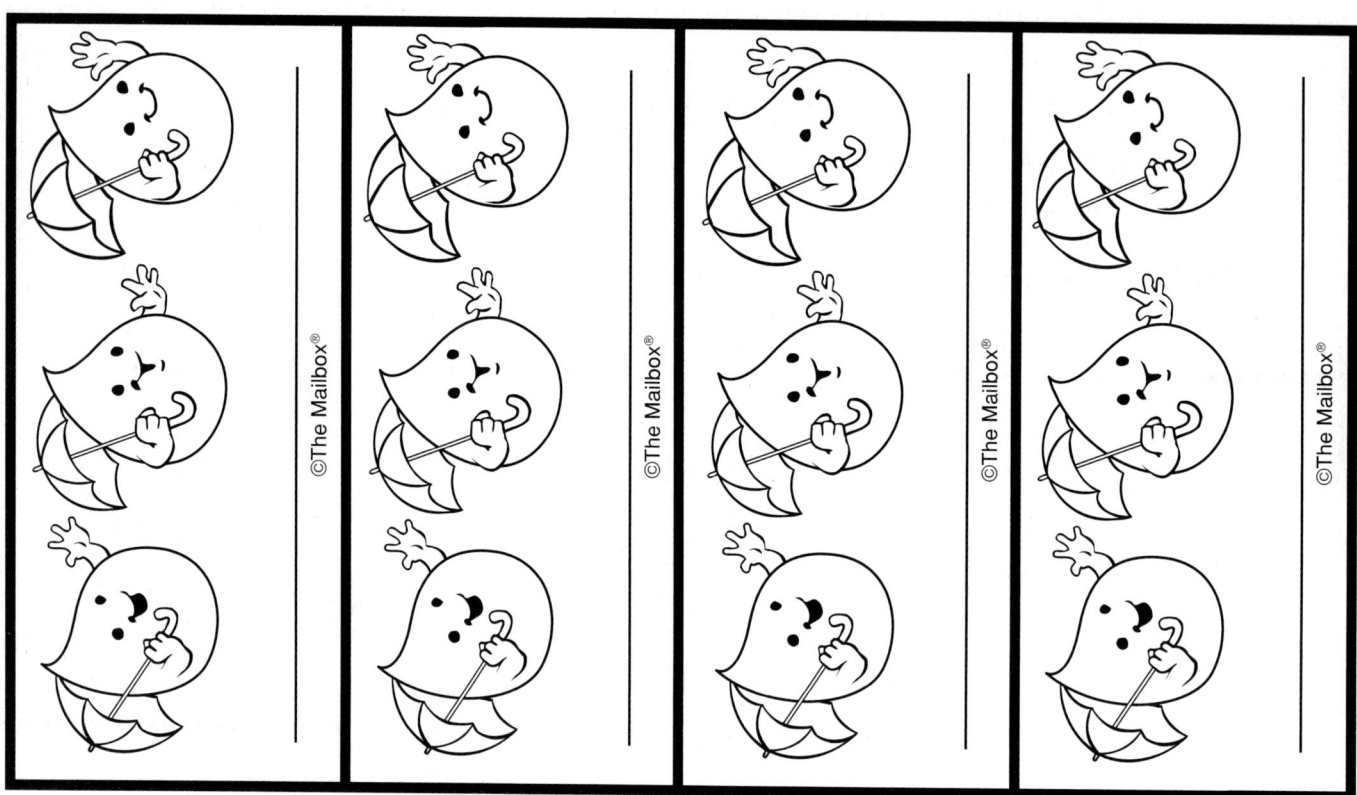

Raindrop Patterns
Use with "Ready for Raindrops" on page 16 and "Letter Cloudburst" on page 17.

Picture Cards
Use with "Picture a Rainy Day" on page 15.

Booklet Cover and Page 1
Use with "Who Needs Rain?" on page 16.

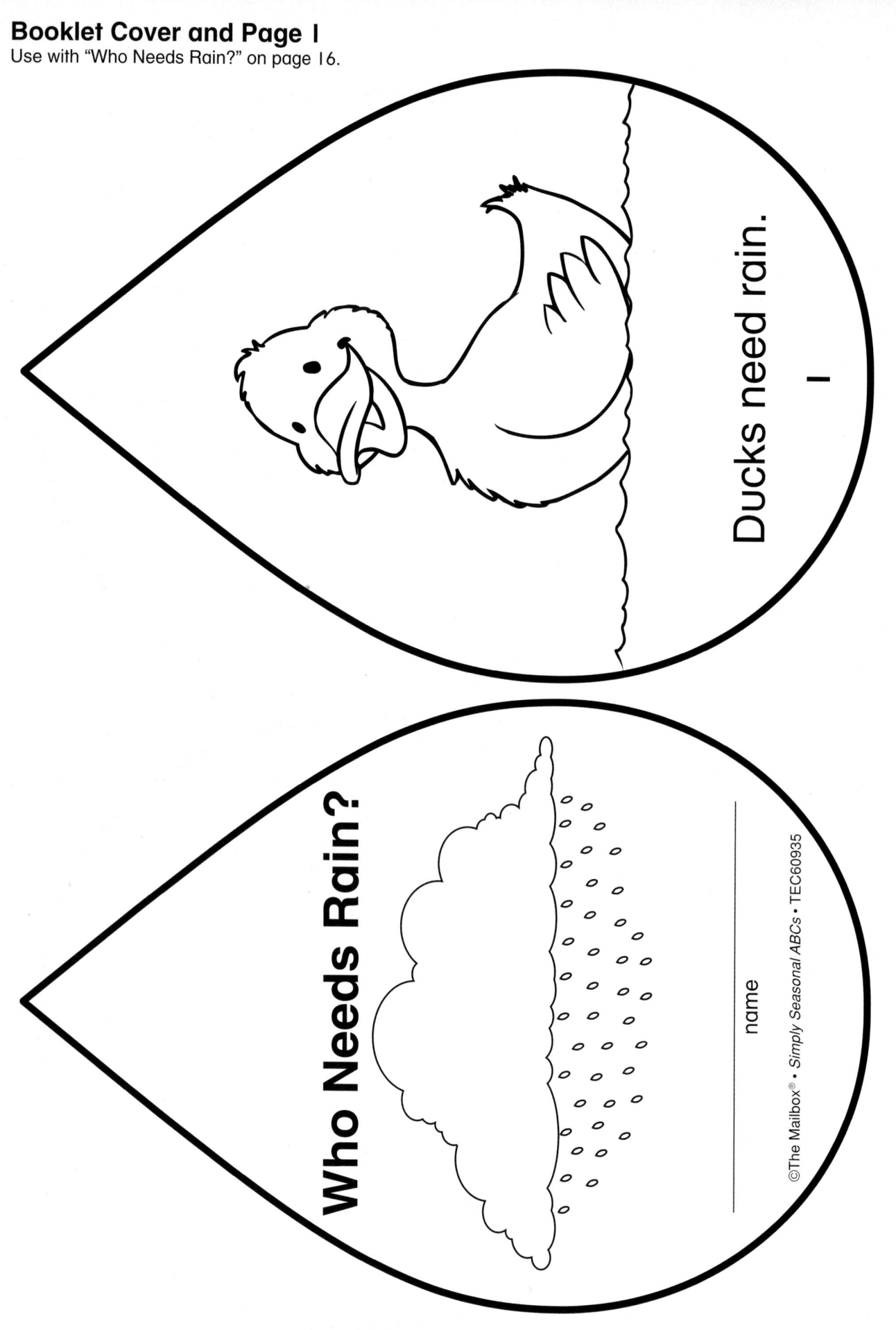

Booklet Pages 2 and 3
Use with "Who Needs Rain?" on page 16.

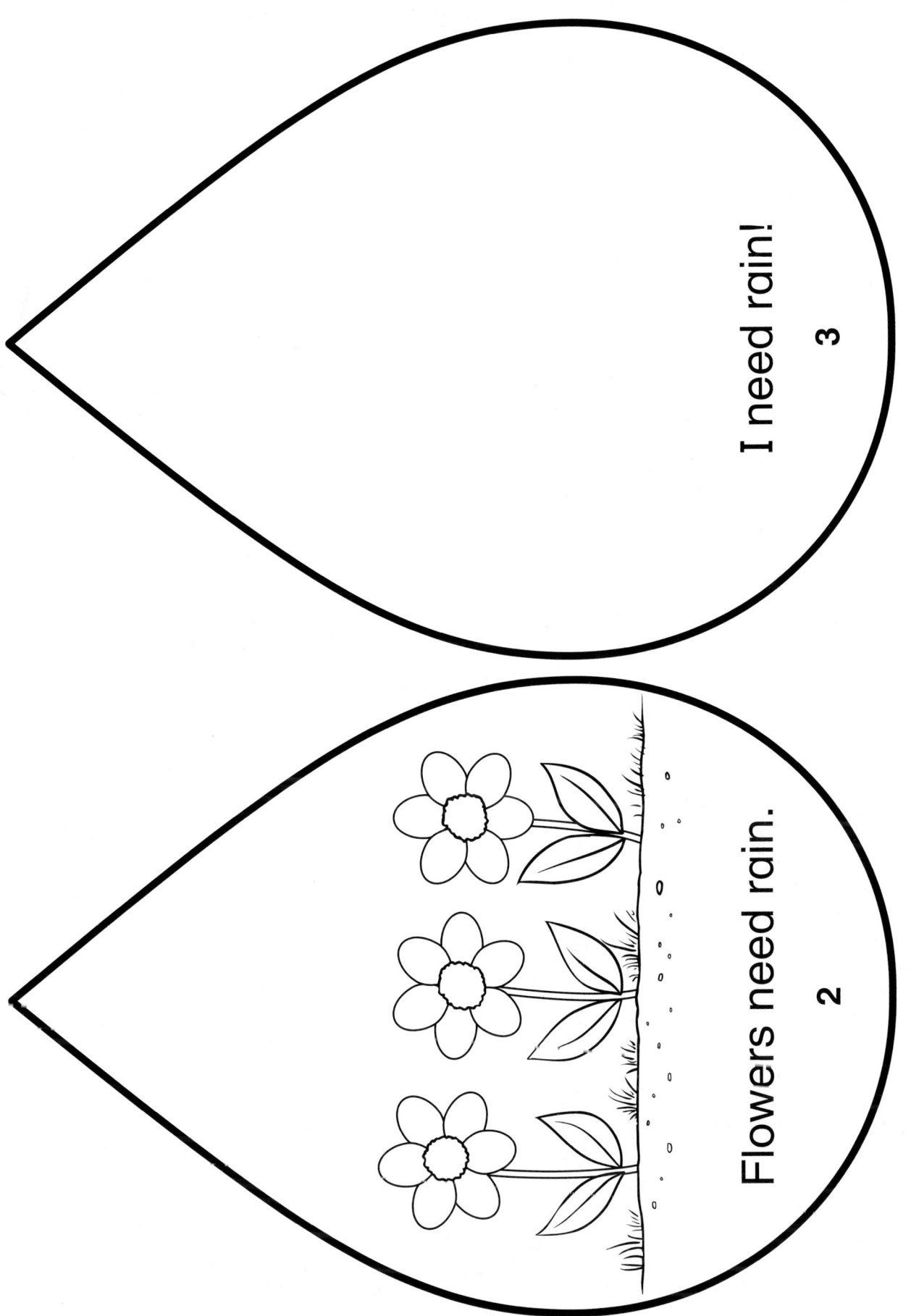

Name _____

Sequencing

Ready for Rain

🖍 Color. ✂ Cut. 🧴 Glue in order.

| 1 | 2 | 3 | 4 |

©The Mailbox® • Simply Seasonal ABCs • TEC60935

Rr

J Is for Jelly Bean!

Jelly Bean Jump
Recognizing initial sound /j/

Here's an energetic way to reinforce the sound of the letter *J*! Have students stand in a circle. Explain that when you say a word that begins with /j/, as in *jelly bean,* they should jump once in place. If your word does not begin with a /j/ sound, students should remain still and wait to hear the next word. Slowly say some words that begin with /j/ and some that do not (see the list for /j/ word suggestions). Get ready to get the wiggles out!

jump	jungle	just
jeep	jacket	jewelry
jar	jug	jolly
junk	jam	jelly
jeans	jet	jaw

Jeans!

Bean Letters
Forming the letter *J*

Jelly beans are just right for some letter *J* practice! Gather several jelly bean rubber stamps and an assortment of washable ink pads. Program a sheet of paper with a large uppercase and lowercase *J;* then copy it to make a class supply. Place the sheets, stamps, and ink pads in a center. A child visits the center and stamps jelly beans along the letters on his paper.

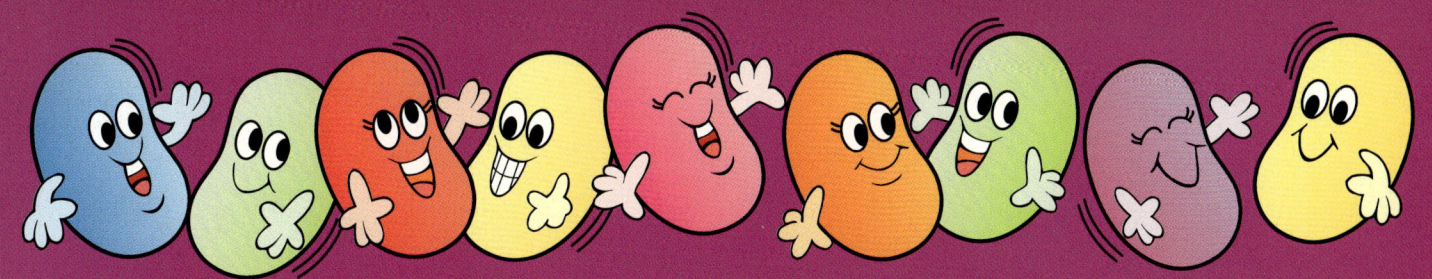

Puzzle Beans
Matching uppercase and lowercase letters

Make a match with this fun partner game! To prepare, use the pattern on page 27 to make several colorful construction paper jelly bean cutouts. Program each jelly bean with a different uppercase and lowercase letter pair. Laminate the jelly beans for durability if desired. Then use a different puzzle cut to separate each letter pair. Mix up the halves and place them at a center. Have a pair of youngsters match the jelly bean halves. For an additional challenge, encourage students to place the assembled jelly beans in alphabetical order. Now that's a sweet job!

A Sweet Booklet
Recognizing associations between spoken and printed words

Oh, boy—jelly beans! Reading about them in this cute booklet is *almost* as good as eating them! Copy pages 28 and 29 to make a class supply. Give each child a set of copies and help him cut out the cover and booklet pages. Assist him in stacking the pages in order behind the cover; then staple the booklet along the left side. If desired, invite him to color the pictures. Read the booklet aloud with him, encouraging him to track the print with his finger as you read. Then invite the child to read the booklet with a partner.

Jelly Bean Lotto
Identifying letters

Sweeten your students' letter identification skills with this small-group game! To prepare, copy the game cards on page 30 to make enough for a small group. Next, randomly program each card with alphabet letters. If desired, lightly color the jelly beans and then laminate the cards for durability. Give each child a card and a handful of paper squares to use as markers. To begin play, call out a letter (making sure to write it down for later card checking). If a child has the letter on her card, she covers it with a marker. The first child to cover all of her squares announces, "Jelly beans!" to end the round. Then check the child's card and play again.

"Bean" Looking for /J/?
Identifying initial consonant sounds

Try this activity to build beginning sound awareness! Copy the jelly bean cards on page 31 onto construction paper. Cut apart the cards and store them in a basket. Gather a small group of students. Help each child, in turn, draw a card, identify the object in the picture, and say the object's initial sound. If the picture's name begins with /j/, the child places the card in a pile. If it begins with another letter sound, the child places the card in a different pile. Continue in this manner until all the cards have been sorted.

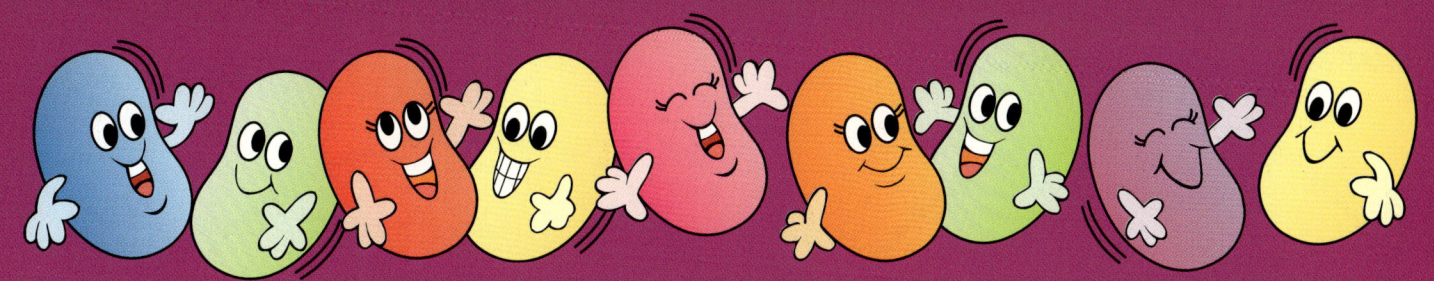

Jelly Bean Colors
Identifying color words

A rousing rendition of this colorful song is lots of fun! Use the pattern below to make eight jelly bean cutouts on white construction paper. Using a corresponding marker, program each cutout with a different color word from the song below. Display the cutouts. Next, teach youngsters the song, pointing to the matching color word as it is sung. Then give each of eight students a cutout. As the class sings the song, have each student hold up her jelly bean when appropriate. Repeat the activity until each child has had a turn.

(sung to the tune of "Jingle Bells")

Jelly beans,
Jelly beans,
Lots of color fun.
Purple, orange, pink, and blue—
I like every one!

Jelly beans,
Jelly beans,
Colors bright and true.
Red, yellow, black, and green—
All for me and you!

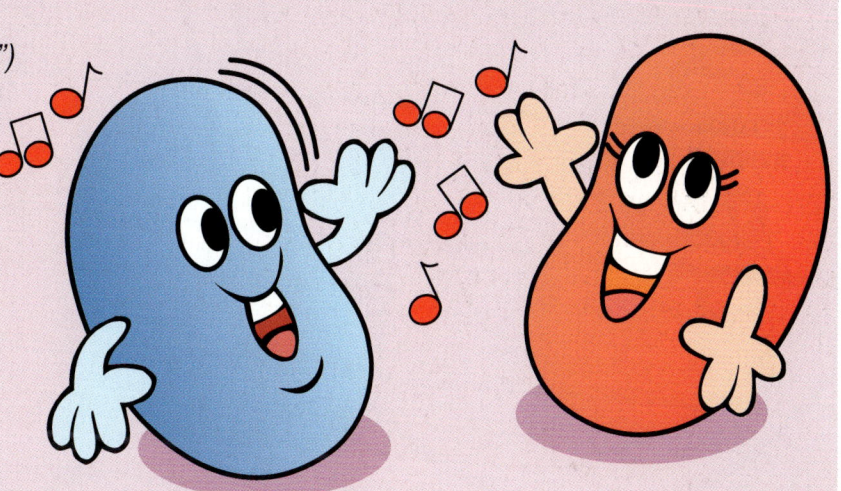

Jelly Bean Pattern
Use with "Puzzle Beans" on page 25 and "Jelly Bean Colors" above.

Booklet Cover and Pages 1–2
Use with "A Sweet Booklet" on page 25.

Jelly Beans!

Name

Jelly beans are bright.

1

Jelly beans are sweet.

2

Booklet Pages 3–4
Use with "A Sweet Booklet" on page 25.

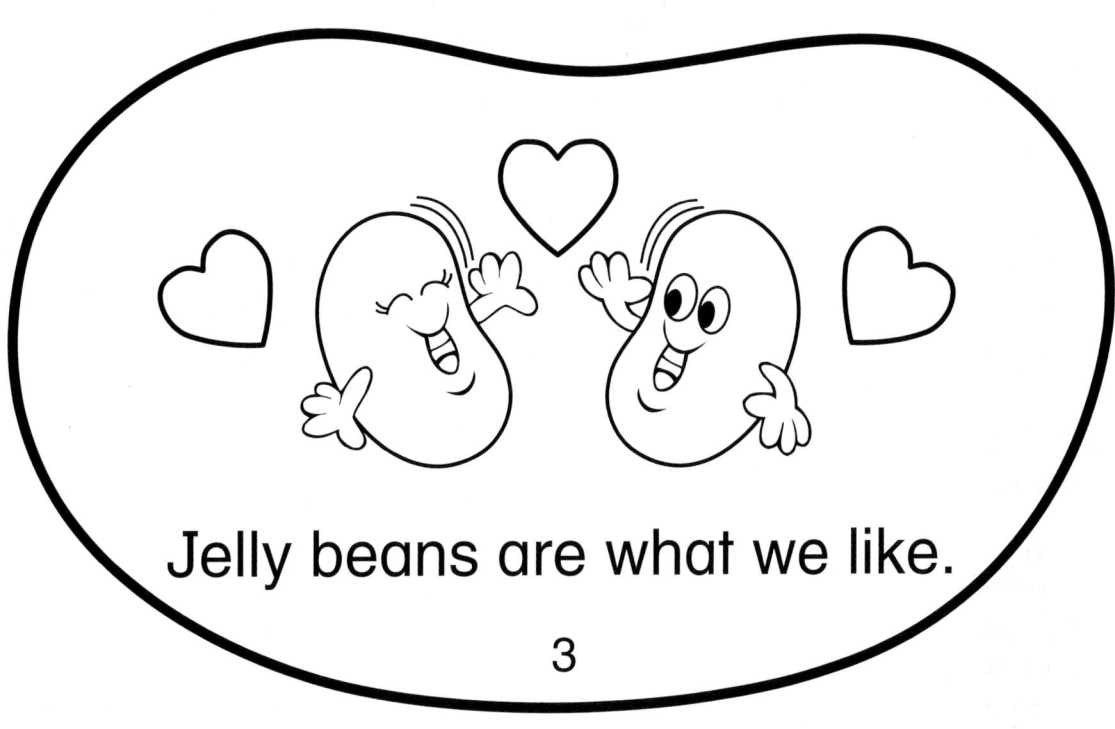

Jelly beans are what we like.

3

They are really good to eat!

4

Lotto Cards
Use with "Jelly Bean Lotto" on page 26.

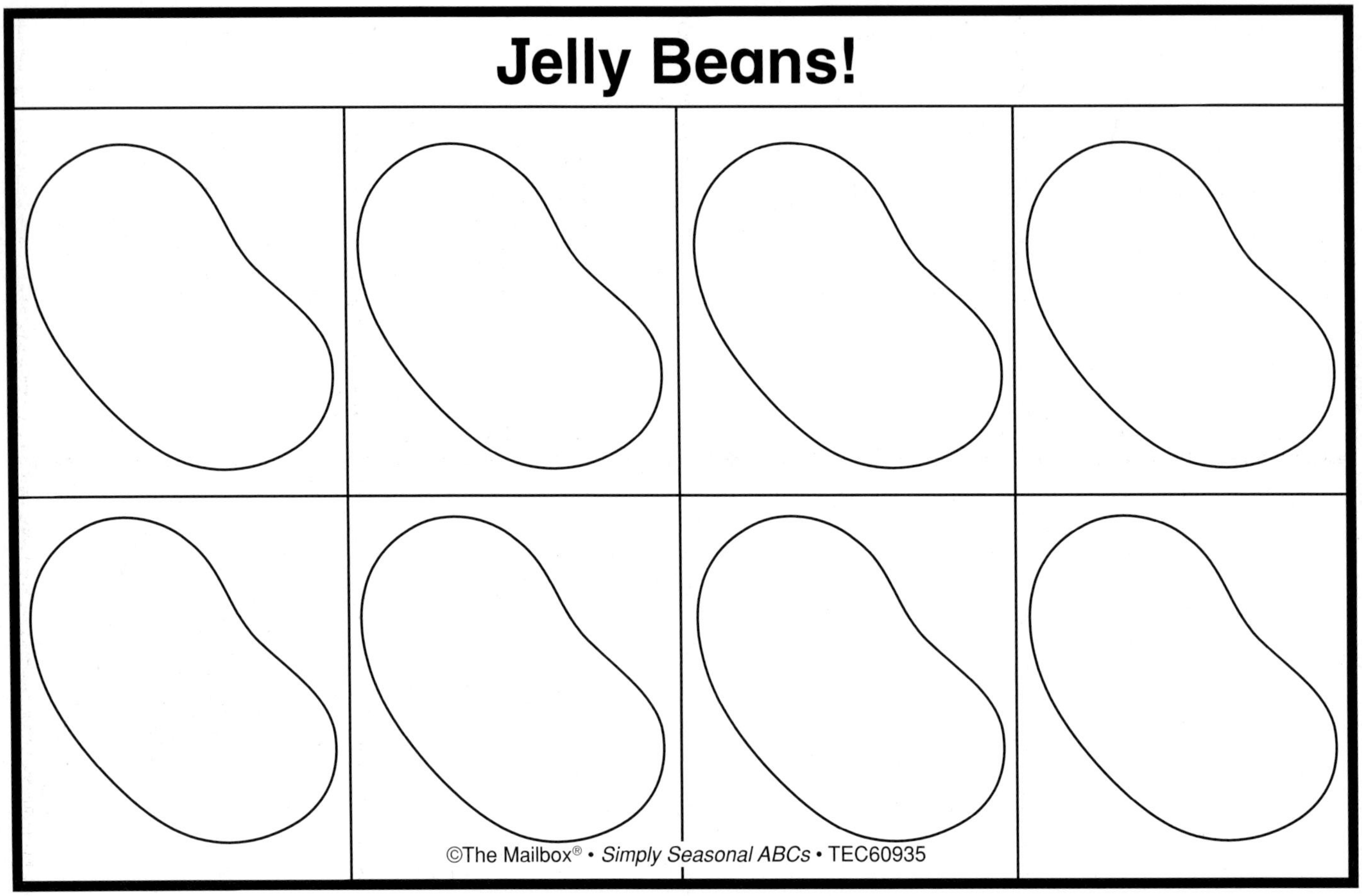

Jelly Beans!

©The Mailbox® • *Simply Seasonal ABCs* • TEC60935

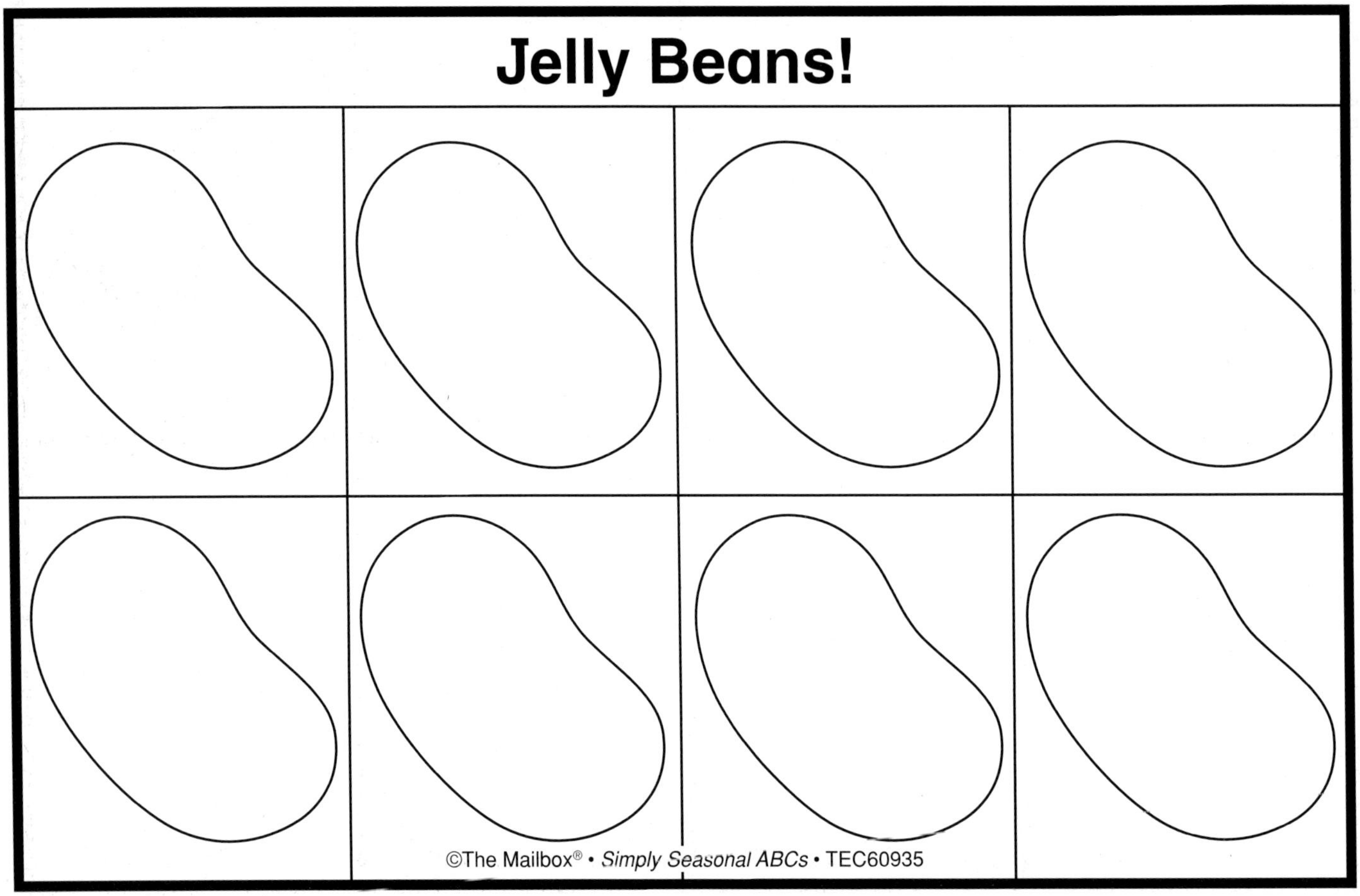

Jelly Beans!

©The Mailbox® • *Simply Seasonal ABCs* • TEC60935

Jelly Bean Cards
Use with "'Bean' Looking for /J/?" on page 26.

Big Beans

- Color the rhyming pictures.
- Draw an X on the one that does not belong.

Jj

D Is for Duck!

Darling Ducks
Recognizing initial sound /d/

Here's a delightful way to help youngsters recognize words that begin with /d/! Give each student half of a small paper plate, a craft feather, and a yellow construction paper cutout of the duck head on page 38. Have each youngster paint one side of the plate yellow. When the paint is dry, instruct him to print an uppercase and a lowercase *D* on the plate. Then direct him to glue the head and feather to the plate, as shown, to resemble a duck. To begin, say a word aloud. If the word begins with /d/, each student holds up his duck and says the /d/ sound. If it does not begin with /d/, he does not hold up his duck. Continue in this manner for several other words. Now that's a phonemic awareness activity that is just ducky!

Paddle Around the Pond
Recognizing rhyming words

"Quacking" up is half the fun when little ones help a hungry duckling get to its food! To make a gameboard, program a sheet of blue poster board as shown. Gather a small group of students around the gameboard. Place a small rubber duck or duck cutout in the upper left-hand corner. To play, say several pairs of words. When the words in a pair rhyme, the students quack like ducks and then a volunteer moves the duck to the next marked space on the board. When the words do not rhyme, the students remain silent and the duck is not moved. The game is over when the duck reaches the plants, where it can fill its tummy. What a lucky ducky!

Just Ducky Spelling
Using left-to-right progression

Little ones are sure to delight in matching letters from left to right with this center activity! Use the duck pattern on page 38 to make several yellow construction paper ducks. Program each duck with a simple thematic word such as *duck, swim, pond,* or *dive;* then laminate the ducks and cut them out. Next, attach a strip of magnetic tape to the back of each duck. Place the ducks, a set of magnetic letters, and a magnetic board at a center. When a youngster visits the center, she chooses a duck and places it on the magnetic board. Then she spells the word from left to right by finding the matching letters and placing them below the duck. After she spells the word, she points to each letter, from left to right, and names it. No doubt your little ducklings will flock to this center again and again!

Pass the Duck
Naming words that begin with /d/

A rubber or plush duck and some music are all you need to play this fast-paced circle-time game! Gather students in a circle and hand one student the duck. Instruct students to pass the duck around the circle while you play music. When you stop the music, have the youngster holding the duck name a word that begins with /d/. Play several rounds in this manner until each student has had a turn to say a word that begins with /d/.

Where Is the Duck?
Using positional words in oral language

This class activity provides a great opportunity for little ones to practice using positional words. Invite a student volunteer to hide a rubber or plush duck in the classroom while the other students close their eyes. After the duck is hidden, ask students to open their eyes. Then have the volunteer give a clue about the duck's location using positional words, such as "The duck is below the easel." Invite another student to locate the duck. Once the duck is found, continue the game by having other students take turns hiding and finding the duck. Your fine-feathered flock is sure to fancy this activity!

At the Pond
Sorting uppercase and lowercase letters

Make a splash with letter sorting using this dandy center! Obtain two large plastic containers and a supply of plastic or rubber ducks that float. Use a permanent marker to program the bottom of each duck with an uppercase or a lowercase letter. Label one container with an uppercase *D* and the other with a lowercase *D*. Partially fill the containers with blue-tinted water. Then place the containers, the ducks, and a towel at a center. When a youngster visits the center, she chooses a duck and identifies the letter on its underside as uppercase or lowercase. Then she places the duck in the corresponding container. She continues in this manner until all the ducks are sorted. To clean up, she removes the ducks from the water and places them on a towel.

A Duck Tale
Tracking print

The predictable text in this booklet is just right for little ones to follow along with the print! Make a copy of the duck pattern on page 38 and the booklet cover and pages on pages 39–40 for each student. Have each youngster color the duck and the booklet pages and then cut them out. Sequence the pages and staple them atop the duck cutout for each child. Give each youngster a craft feather to use as a pointer. Read the text aloud while each student follows along, pointing to each word. After a few readings, invite little ones to read their booklets with a partner while pointing to each word. Then encourage them to take their booklets and feathers home to share the duck tale with their families!

Ducks in a Row
Using alphabetical order

How do little ones get these ducks in a row? By arranging them in alphabetical order of course! Reduce the duck pattern on page 38 and make 26 yellow construction paper copies. Program each duck with a different letter and then cut it out. Store the ducks in a resealable plastic bag. Place the bag at a center along with an alphabet chart. Have two students work together to arrange the ducks in an alphabetical row, referring to the chart as needed. Once the ducks are all lined up, have the two students check the order by singing the alphabet song as they point to each duck.

Duck Head Pattern
Use with "Darling Ducks" on page 34.

Duck Pattern
Use with "Just Ducky Spelling" on page 35, "A Duck Tale" on page 37, and "Ducks in a Row" on page 37.

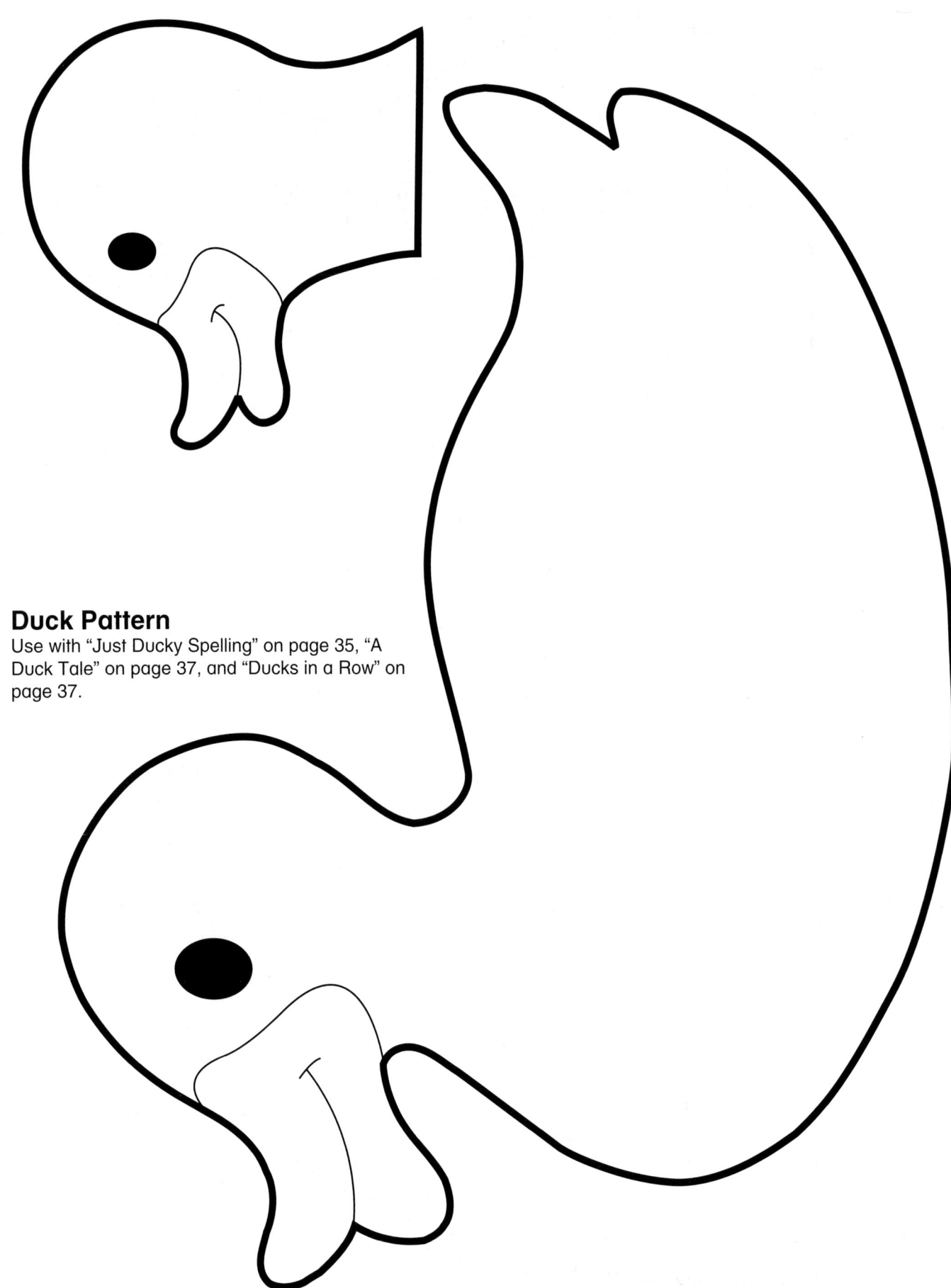

Booklet Cover and Page 1
Use with "A Duck Tale" on page 37.

A Duck Tale

by _____

©The Mailbox® • Simply Seasonal ABCs • TEC60935

The duck can swim.

1

Booklet Pages
Use with "A Duck Tale" on page 37.

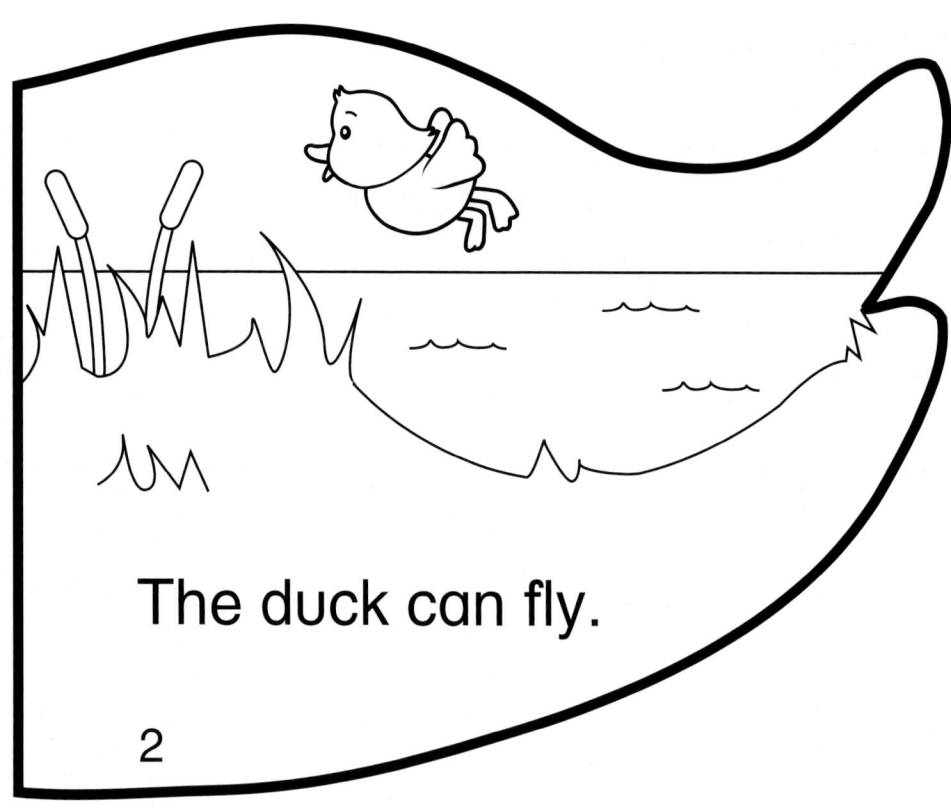

The duck can fly.

2

The duck can dance.
Oh my!

3

Name _____   Visual Discrimination

All "Quacked" Up!

🖍 Color by the code.

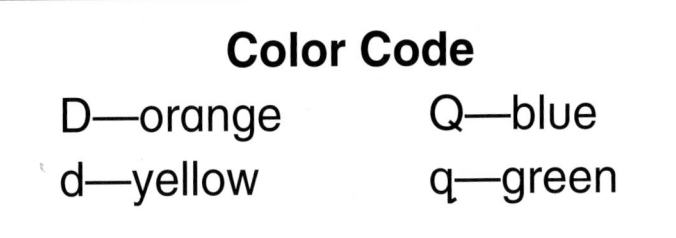

Color Code	
D—orange	Q—blue
d—yellow	q—green

©The Mailbox® • Simply Seasonal ABCs • TEC60935

Name _____ Initial Sound /d/

Visiting Friends

Help Duck get to his friends.

🖍 Color each picture that begins like *duck*.

Dd

M Is for Mother!

Mother, May I?
Recognizing words with initial sound /m/

What better way to provide practice with recognizing words that begin with /m/ than with a fun-filled game? Have students imagine that they are babies and you are the mother. Then, in an open area of the classroom or outside, direct youngsters to stand in a line side by side. Stand about five feet from the line, facing the students. Say a familiar word. If the word begins with /m/, like *mother,* students take one step toward you. If the word does not begin with /m/, they take one step away from you. Play continues until all of the babies reach you—the mother!

Letter Match
Recognizing and sorting the letters M and B

Little ones are sure to enjoy playing the roles of mothers and babies during this sorting activity! Program one sheet of poster board with a large *M* for *mother* and another sheet with a large *B* for *baby.* Display the posters within students' reach. Program a class supply of blank cards with *M*s and *B*s in various sizes, fonts, and colors. Store the cards in a small paper bag. Invite a youngster to remove a card from the bag and name the letter. If the letter is an *M,* instruct him to *walk* to the corresponding letter poster and tape on the card. If the letter is a *B,* have him *crawl* to the corresponding letter poster and tape on the card. Continue in this manner until all of the cards have been sorted.

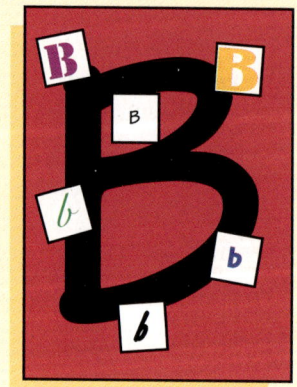

Name That Baby!
Using vocabulary to complete sentences

It's a match—a mom and baby match, that is—with this pocket chart activity. Program a sentence strip with "A _____ is a mom for a _____." Place the strip in a pocket chart. Copy and cut out the mom and baby animal cards on page 48. Place the baby cards below the sentence strip and place the mom cards in a pile next to the pocket chart.

Gather youngsters around the pocket chart and help them name each baby animal. Next, invite a student to choose a mom card from the pile, identify the animal, and place the card on the first blank of the sentence. Point to each word as you read the sentence aloud. Then have a volunteer place the matching baby card on the second blank of the sentence. Encourage little ones to read the resulting sentence along with you. Remove the cards and continue in this manner until each card has been used.

Magnificent M-O-M
Understanding that words are made up of letters

Singing this little ditty is sure to help little ones get in tune with the letters in *mom!* Write each letter in *mom* on a separate sheet of tagboard. Teach youngsters the following song. Then give one letter card to each of three volunteers. Direct them to stand side by side in order. Sing the song while the volunteers hold up their cards at the appropriate times. Repeat the song until each youngster has had a turn to hold a letter card. Mom's the word!

(sung to the tune of "Three Blind Mice")

M-O-M.
M-O-M.
Mom loves her kids.
Mom loves her kids.
She takes good care of her family.
She watches over them carefully.
She makes sure they have the things that they need.
M-O-M!

Family Rhyme Time
Recognizing rhyming words in sentences

Here's a nifty way to provide little ones with rhyming practice! On a chart, write animal-related sentences that include rhyming words, similar to the ones shown. Read a sentence aloud while pointing to each word. Have youngsters listen carefully for the two rhyming words. Invite a volunteer to circle the rhyming words. Then have a different volunteer guess the animal mother and baby described in the sentence. Continue in this manner for the remaining sentences. For an added challenge, encourage youngsters to help you think of more rhyming sentences.

We can (fly) in the (sky).

We can bark at the park.

When we squeak, you may say, "Eek!"

Mud is the best; it's where we rest.

Who Has a Mother?
Connecting to literature

This ready-to-go activity is "write" on! Read aloud *Does a Kangaroo Have a Mother, Too?* by Eric Carle. After reading, have students recall the different animals (mothers and babies) featured in the story. If desired, use the list in the back of the book to teach youngsters the names of the baby animals. Then ask little ones to name other mother and baby animal pairs.

Next, give each student a copy of the writing prompt on page 49. Have her cut off the strip of words from her paper. Then direct her to choose a baby animal word, cut it from the strip, and glue it in the space provided. Help each youngster read her sentence. Then encourage her to draw a picture of the animal baby with its mother. Bind students' work between two construction paper covers to make a delightful class book!

A [joey] has a mother.
by Brittany

What's at the End?
Matching ending sounds

Use this small-group activity to provide practice with ending sounds. Invite youngsters to name a few animal mom and baby pairs. Choose one animal pair whose names have different ending sounds. Emphasize the different ending sounds and prepare a chart similar to the one shown. Then say a word that ends with one of the chosen ending sounds. Instruct youngsters to carefully listen to the ending sound in the named word. Then invite a volunteer to match the word's ending sound to the ending sound in one of the animal names. Record his response on the chart. Ask a different student to circle the ending sound of the word. Continue in this manner for several words. What a great way to practice phonemic awareness skills!

cat	kitten
ha(t)	pa(n)
si(t)	ru(n)
we(t)	

Some Big, Some Small
Recognizing opposites

Making this unique booklet helps youngsters recognize opposites! For each student, make a copy of pages 50 and 51. Have each youngster cut out each booklet page along the solid lines. Then help him cut on the dotted lines within the text of booklet pages 1 through 3. Sequence the pages and staple them behind the cover. Read aloud the text as students follow along. During a second reading, invite little ones to identify the opposite words on pages 1 through 4. Then invite youngsters to color the pictures and draw a desired mom and baby picture on page 5. Encourage students to read their booklets with a partner and identify the opposites on each page.

Mom and Baby Animal Cards
Use with "Name That Baby!" on page 45.

A [ ] has a mother.

by _____

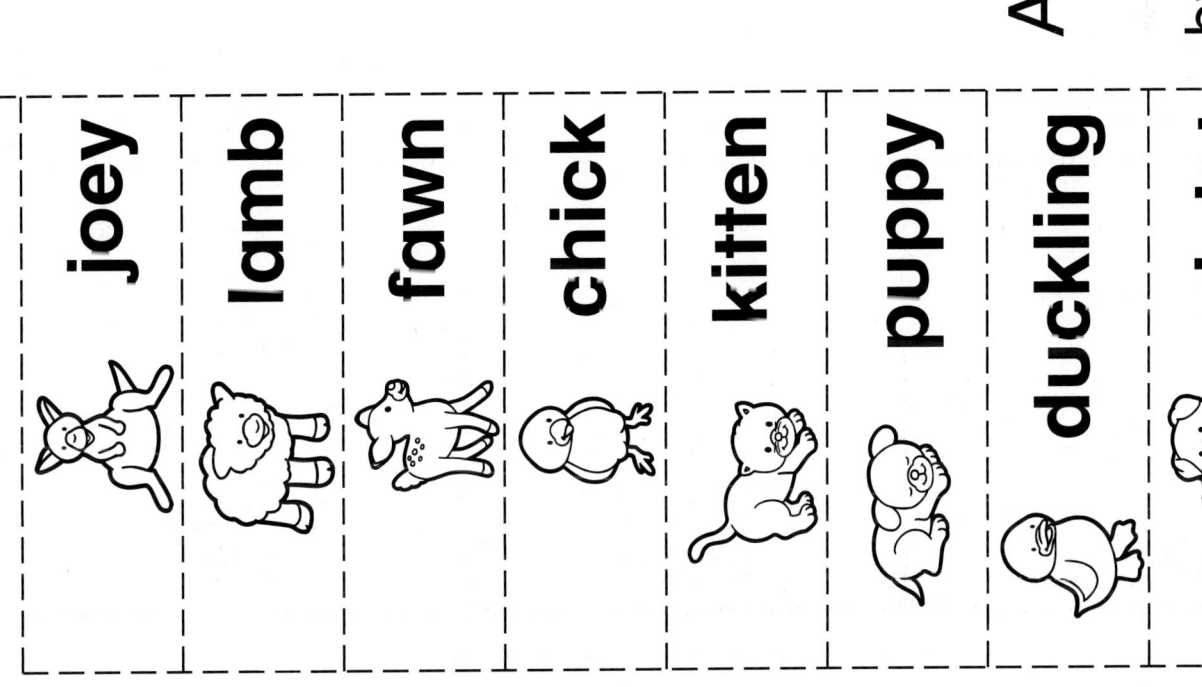

- joey
- lamb
- fawn
- chick
- kitten
- puppy
- duckling
- piglet

Booklet Cover and Pages 1–2
Use with "Some Big, Some Small" on page 47.

Moms and Babies

by _____

©The Mailbox® • Simply Seasonal ABCs • TEC60935

1

big.   little.

2

awake.   asleep.

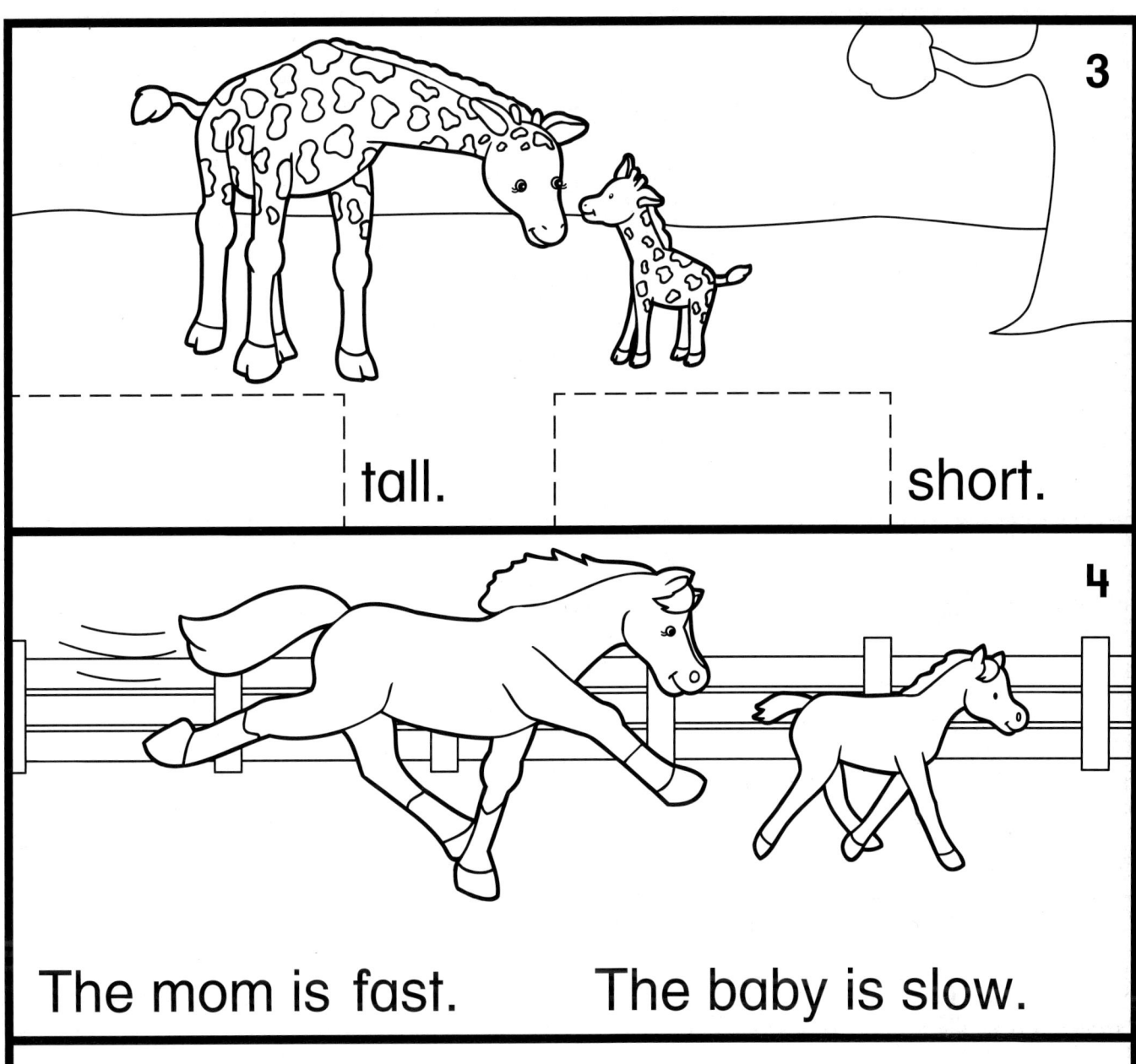

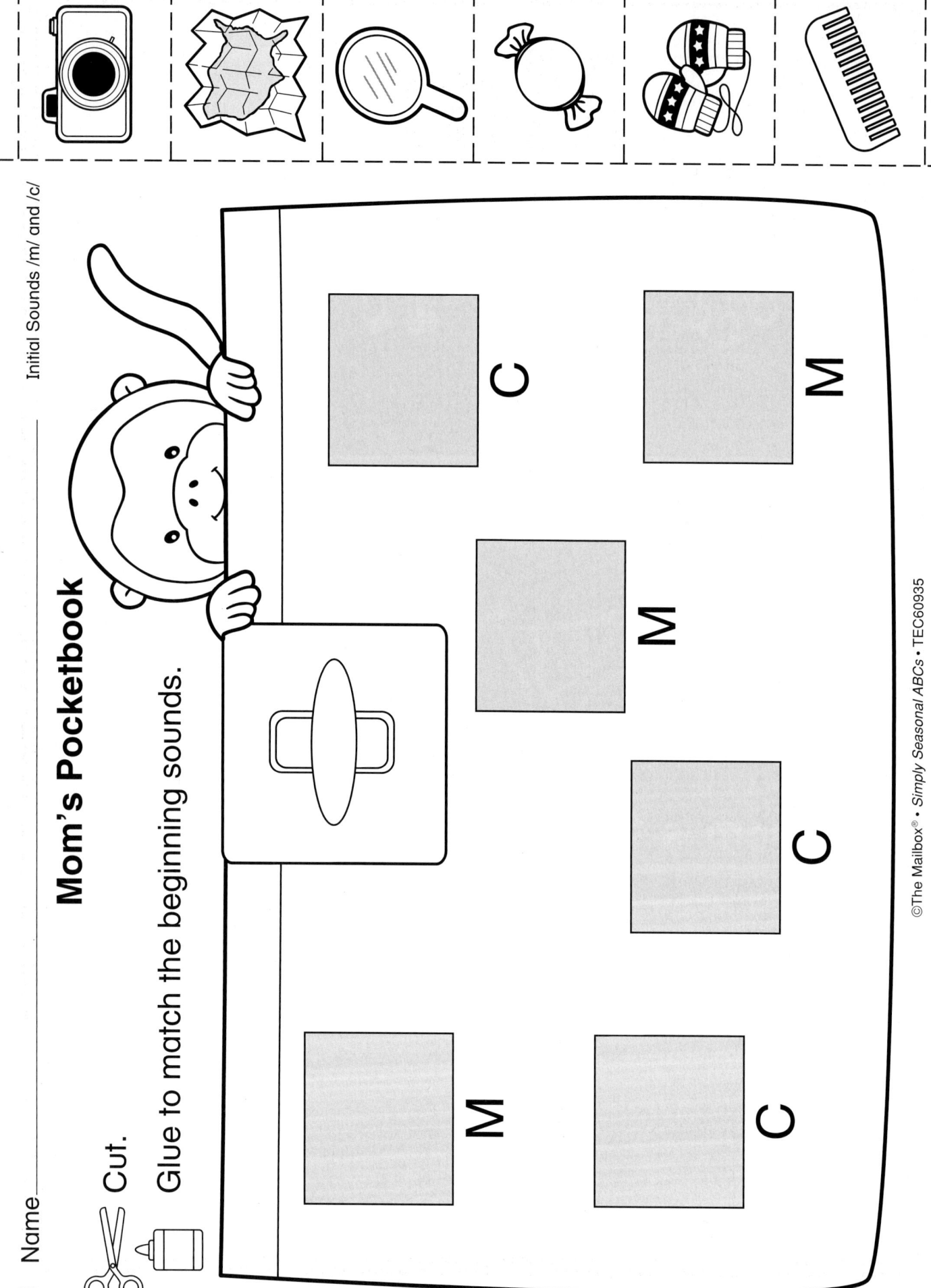

 # Mm

N Is for Nest!

What's in the Nest?
Listening for the initial sound /n/

The bird that made this nest didn't settle for ordinary building materials. It only chose items that begin with /n/! Roll down the top of a paper grocery bag until it resembles a nest. Place items in the nest that begin with /n/, such as the following: a necktie, a number card, a newspaper, a necklace, a nickel, a bag of noodles, a net, a napkin, and a shaker of nutmeg. Explain that birds' nests are often made from items the bird has found, such as yarn or straw. Then tell students that the bird's nest you have is only made of items that begin with /n/ like the sound at the beginning of the word *nest*. Invite a child to remove one of the items from the nest and identify it. Then have students repeat the name of the item, listening carefully for the /n/ sound at the beginning of the word. Repeat the process for each item in the nest.

A Nest Is Nice
Writing the letter N

With this booklet, youngsters are introduced to two little birds who build a nest in a very convenient location! Have each child color a copy of the booklet cover and pages (pages 58 and 59). Have her write her name on the cover and write an uppercase letter *N* in each space in the booklet title. Then instruct her to write a lowercase *N* in each space on pages 1 through 3. Have her glue paper shreds to the large *N* on each page to resemble a nest. Also instruct her to glue a few shreds to each bird's beak on page 2. When the glue is dry, have each child cut out the pages and stack them in order. Then staple them together along the left-hand side. Help youngsters read their booklets. Then have them take the booklets home to share with their families!

Flap Those Wings!
Recognizing rhyming words

Flap, flap, flap! That's what little ones will be busy doing each time they recognize a pair of rhyming words! Gather students and explain that they are going to pretend to be birds sitting on nests. Next, say a pair of words from the list shown. Encourage students to stand up from their nests and flap their arms like wings if the words rhyme. If the words do not rhyme, the students stay seated. Continue in the same way with each pair of words in the list.

nest/best	wing/sing
bird/feet	beak/weak
worm/dirt	fly/try
tree/see	tweet/meet
feather/weather	flap/map

Picture This!
Recognizing initial sound /n/

Coffee filters make perfect nests for this kid-pleasing activity! Make a copy of the picture cards on page 60 for each child. Give each youngster a white coffee filter and encourage her to paint it brown using watercolor paints. When the paint is dry, have her glue the filter to a 9" x 12" sheet of construction paper. Next, have each child cut out the cards. Encourage her to choose a card and say the name of the picture. Instruct her to glue the card to the nest if it begins with /n/. If it doesn't, have her place the card in a separate pile. Encourage her to repeat the process for each card.

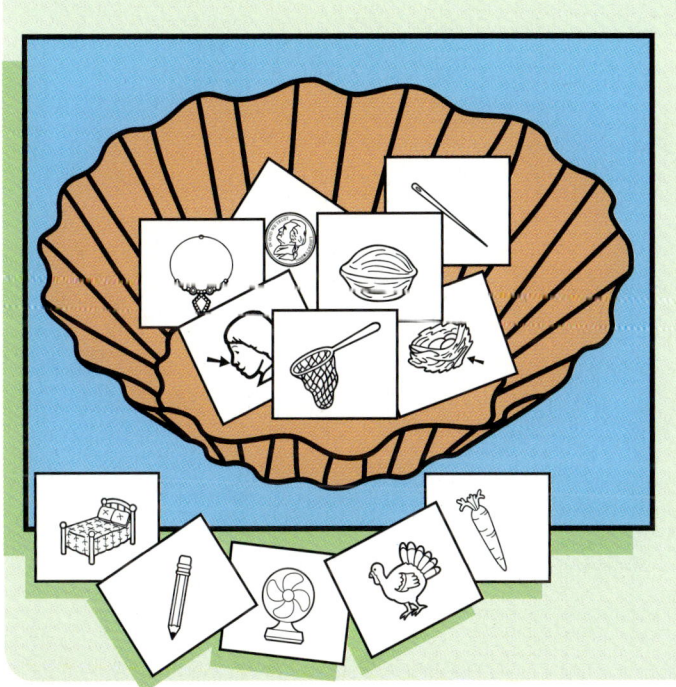

Nest Nibbles
Sequencing pictures

This sequencing activity is a real "tweet"! Make a copy of the sequencing cards on page 61 for each child. To make a snack, encourage each student to place half of a large pretzel rod on a plate. Instruct her to spread chocolate frosting on her pretzel. Have her place several chow mein noodles atop the frosting to resemble a nest. Then invite her to eat her snack. While she is eating, review the steps she used to make her snack. When she is finished, encourage her to color and cut out the cards. Instruct her to place the cards in sequential order on a 6" x 18" strip of paper. After checking the order of her cards, have her glue them in place. Encourage her to take her sequencing strip home to share with her family.

Is It Real?
Distinguishing fantasy from reality

Youngsters distinguish reality from fantasy with this "eggs-tra" fun story-time activity! During separate storytime sessions, read a nonfiction book about nests, such as *A Nest Full of Eggs* by Priscilla Belz Jenkins, and the fiction book *Horton Hatches the Egg* by Dr. Seuss. After each session, have youngsters determine whether the information in the featured book is real or pretend. Ask students to explain their reasoning as you write their comments on chart paper. Little ones will be quick to tell you whether future storytime selections are real or pretend!

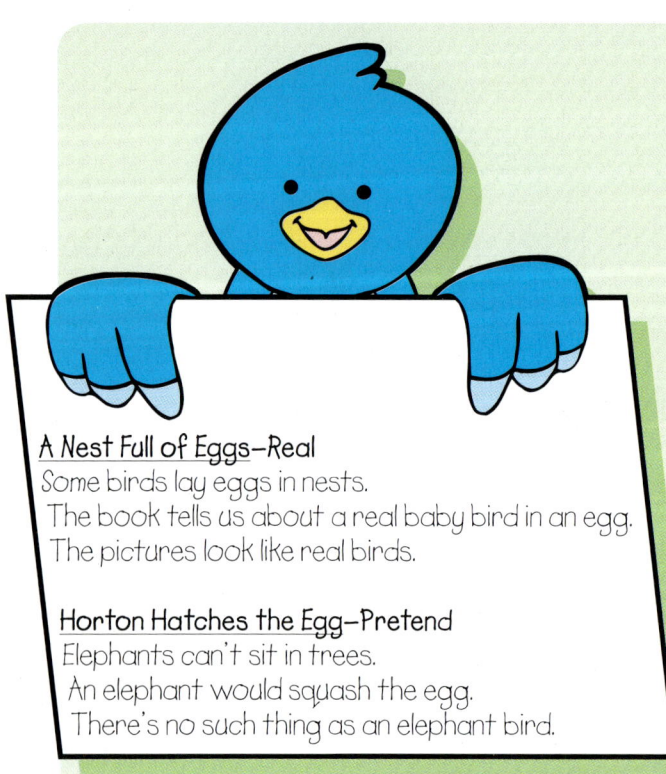

A Nest Full of Eggs—Real
 Some birds lay eggs in nests.
 The book tells us about a real baby bird in an egg.
 The pictures look like real birds.

Horton Hatches the Egg—Pretend
 Elephants can't sit in trees.
 An elephant would squash the egg.
 There's no such thing as an elephant bird.

So Many Colors!
Identifying color words

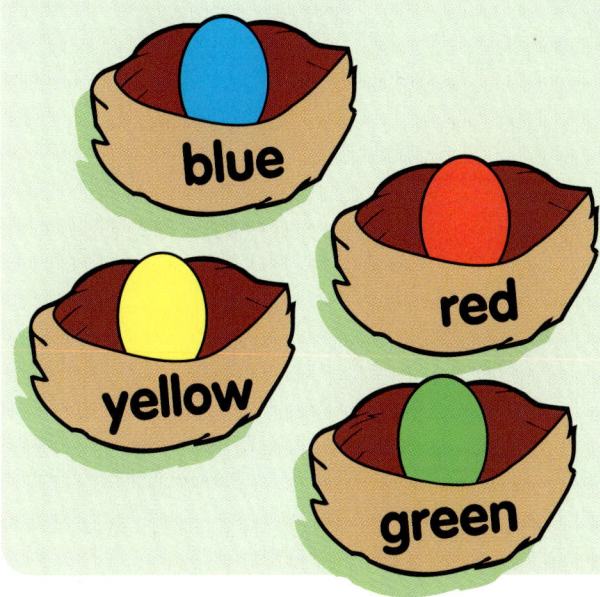

No doubt birds would be extraordinarily proud of these colorful eggs! Make eight tan construction paper copies of the nest pattern on page 60. Then write a different color word on each nest. (Depending on student ability, you may wish to write each color word in its corresponding color.) Make a construction paper egg cutout in each color. Laminate the props for durability and then place them at a center. A youngster visits the center and chooses a nest. After he reads the color word, he places the corresponding egg on the nest. Then he continues in the same way for each remaining nest. Look at all those colorful eggs!

Pass It On
Naming words that begin with /n/

This twist on the traditional game Hot Potato is sure to get youngsters thinking about words that begin with /n/! Make a nest by gluing brown paper shreds to the inside of a paper bowl. When the glue is dry, place several plastic eggs on top of the shreds. Gather youngsters in a circle. Have them sing the song below as they pass the nest around the circle, taking care to keep the eggs in the nest. Have the child holding the nest at the end of the song name a word that begins with /n/ like the word *nest*. (For an easier version, have the student name the sound of the letter *N*.) Then have youngsters sing the song again as they continue to pass the nest.

(sung to the tune of "Do Your Ears Hang Low?")

We will pass the nest,
And we all will do our best
So the eggs don't drop
On the floor and go kerplop.
When this song's done, then
We will sing it all again.
We will pass the nest!

Booklet Cover and Page 1
Use with "A Nest Is Nice" on page 54.

Booklet Pages 2 and 3
Use with "A Nest Is Nice" on page 54.

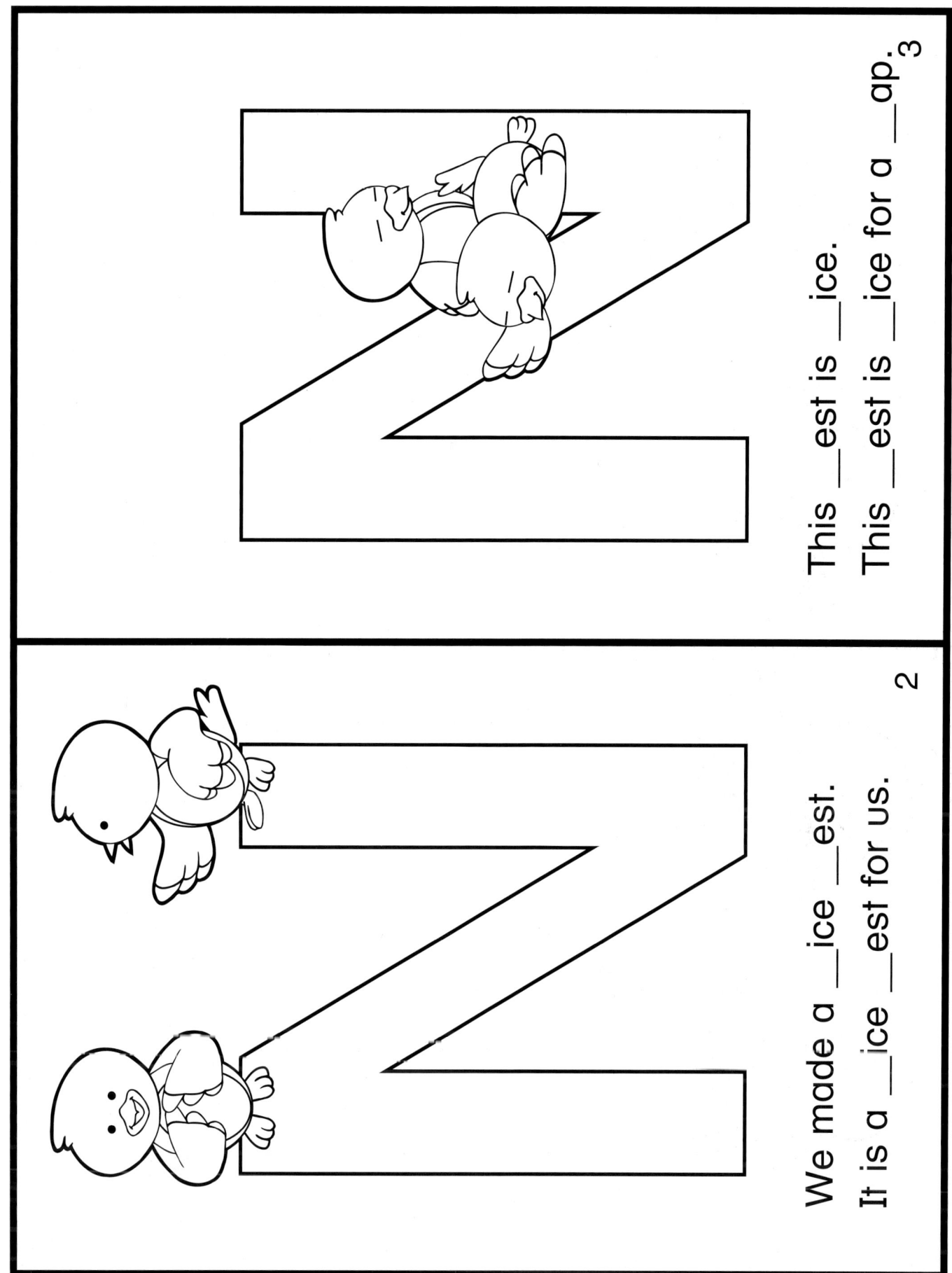

Picture Cards
Use with "Picture This!" on page 55.

Nest Pattern
Use with "So Many Colors!" on page 57.

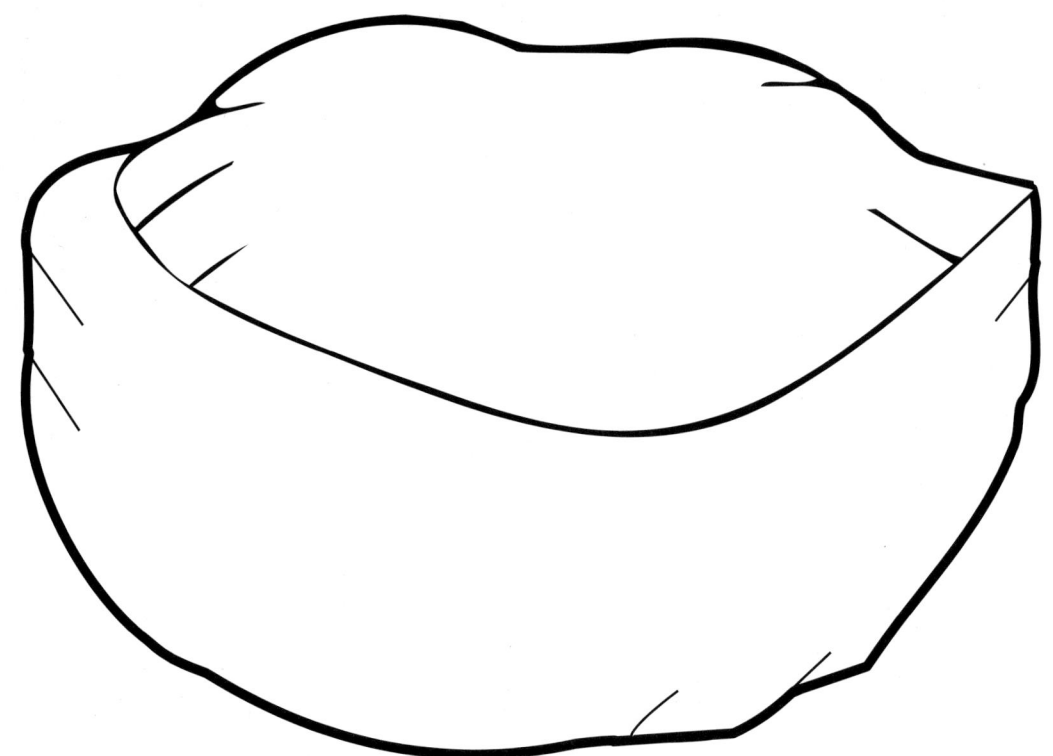

Sequencing Cards
Use with "Nest Nibbles" on page 56.

Name _____ Initial Sound /n/

Proud Papa!

🖍 Color the eggs with pictures that begin with /n/.

62 ©The Mailbox® • Simply Seasonal ABCs • TEC60935

 # Nn

F Is for Farm!

Roundin' Up Fs
Recognizing the letter F

Round up some letter fun with this small-group activity! To prepare, gather blocks or plastic fence pieces. Program a supply of cards with a variety of uppercase and lowercase letters in different sizes, fonts, and colors, making sure to include several *F*s. Laminate the cards, if desired, and store them in a container. To begin, gather four or five students in a circle and have them work together to use the blocks or fence pieces to build a small fence within the circle. After the fence is completed, have each student take a turn drawing a card from the container. Have the student place the card inside the fence if the letter on it is an *F*. Instruct him to place the card outside of the fence if the letter is not *F*. Continue until all the cards have been drawn.

"Egg-ceptional" Letter F!
Identifying initial sound /f/

Scramble up some farm-fresh fun at this letter sorting center! To prepare, gather 24 plastic eggs and two cleaned and sanitized egg cartons. Use a permanent marker to program the inside lid of one carton with "Ff." Write "Other" on the inside lid of the second carton. Duplicate the picture cards on page 68, color and cut them out, and use clear packing tape to attach one card to each egg. Store the programmed eggs in a plastic tub filled with raffia to represent a nest. Then place the nest and the opened egg cartons at a center. When a child visits the center, he takes an egg from the nest, says the pictured word, and places the egg in the correct carton. He continues in this manner with the remaining eggs. Your students will rate this center Grade A!

Where's the Farmer?
Matching printed words to words in a song

Rise and shine! This little ditty about a farmer's busy day will help your youngsters match words and pictures to song lyrics. Color a copy of the cards on page 69, cut them apart, and then glue a craft stick to the back of each card. Gather a group of four students. Direct students' attention to the word on each card. Read the word aloud and have students identify the initial letter and its sound. Then give each child a card. Sing the song below and encourage each child to hold up his card as its verse is sung. Then invite youngsters to sing along as they continue to hold up their cards when appropriate. What a busy farmer!

(sung to the tune of "The More We Get Together")

The farmer's in the barn, the barn, the barn.
The farmer's in the barn; now what does he see?
A pink pig, a brown horse, and a black cow, of course—
The farmer's in the barn, and that's what he sees.

The farmer's in the field, the field, the field.
The farmer's in the field; now what does he see?
A tractor, some tall wheat, and yellow corn so sweet—
The farmer's in the field, and that's what he sees.

The farmer's in the yard, the yard, the yard.
The farmer's in the yard; now what does he see?
A white goose, a small duck, and some chickens that cluck—
The farmer's in the yard, and that's what he sees!

A Funny Farm
Identifying rhyming words

Your youngsters will laugh until the cows come home after reading these rhyming booklets! Give each youngster a copy of the barn pattern on page 67 and the booklet cover and pages on page 70. Have him color the pages and cut them out. Next, help him sequence his pages and staple them atop the door of the barn. Read the booklet aloud and have students follow along and underline the rhyming words on each page. Then invite students to read along with you, making sure to emphasize the rhyming words.

A Crop of Letters
Matching uppercase and lowercase letters

Hay isn't just for horses at this letter-matching center! Use the patterns on page 68 to make several copies of the tractor on one color of construction paper and the same number of hay-filled wagons on a different color of construction paper. Use a marker to write a different uppercase letter on each tractor and its matching lowercase letter on a wagon of hay. Cut out the cards and laminate them if desired. Store the cards in a paper bag decorated with a copy of the barn pattern on page 67 and place it at a center. Invite a student to remove the cards and sort them by color. Next, have her match the uppercase and lowercase letters until each tractor is paired with its corresponding wagon. When she has finished, have the student place the tractors and wagons back in the bag for easy cleanup. Happy farming!

Patch 'em Up!
Using rimes to read words

These jolly scarecrows won't scare your youngsters away from word family practice! Use an overhead projector to enlarge two copies of the scarecrow pattern (page 71) onto separate sheets of poster board; then color and laminate them if desired. Program each sheet of poster board with a different rime and post it within students' reach. For each of the two rimes, program a supply of construction paper patches with a different word that includes the rime. Place the patches inside a container and mix them up. Read the rimes on the scarecrows aloud. Have each student, in turn, randomly draw a patch. Have her underline the rime and then help her read the word. Next, instruct her to use a loop of tape to attach the patch to the corresponding scarecrow. Once the scarecrows are all patched up, invite youngsters to read the words for additional practice.

Once Upon a Farmyard
Identifying and using describing words

Here's a hilarious class book project that students are sure to graze through again and again! Share a farm book that contains several describing words, such as *Big Red Barn* by Margaret Wise Brown or *Over on the Farm* by Christopher Gunson. During a second retelling, enlist students' help in identifying describing words and animals in the story. Write students' responses on a chart like the one shown. Also encourage students to brainstorm describing words that are not in the book. Next, have each student create a silly farm animal by choosing one word from each column. Then have him copy the chosen describing words from the chart onto a sheet of paper, providing help as needed. Have him draw a picture to illustrate the animal. Bind students' work between two covers and title the book "Once Upon a Farmyard."

Size	Color	Animal
big	red	pig
little	green	horse
giant	pink	sheep
tiny	white	donkey
	brown	chick

big green chick

Barn Pattern
Use with "A Funny Farm" on page 65 and "A Crop of Letters" on page 66.

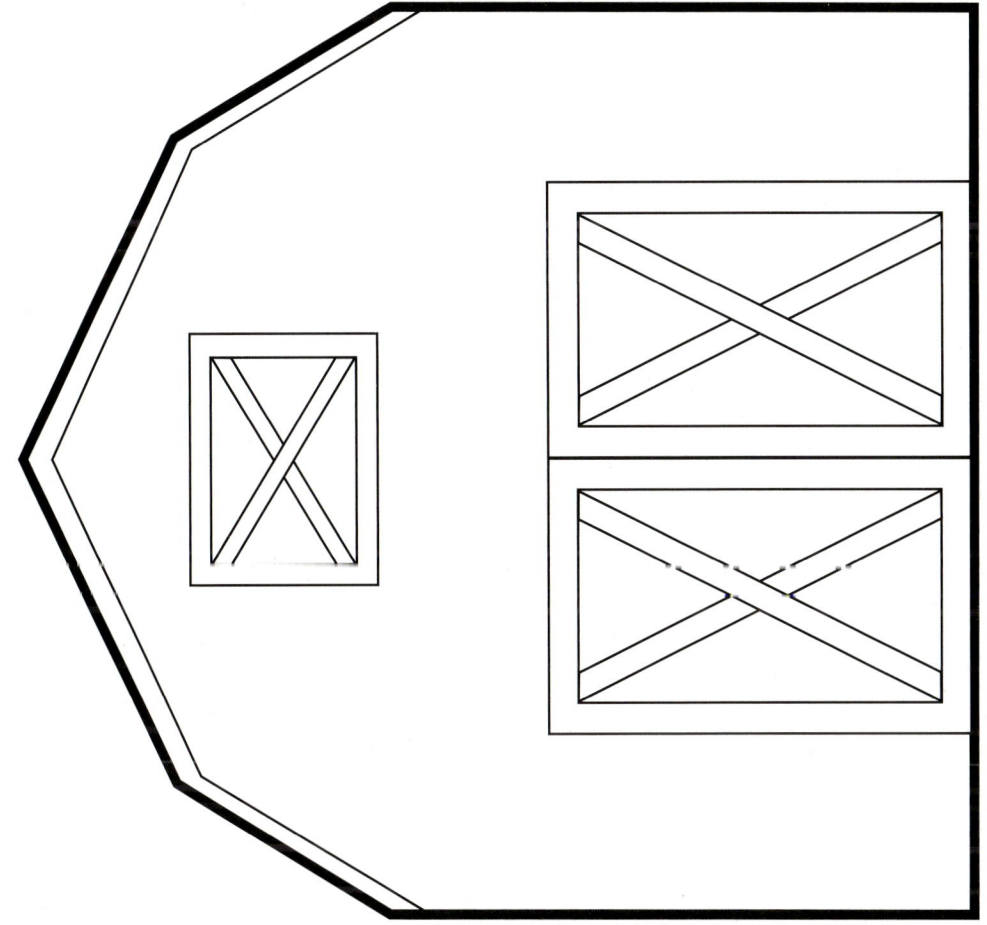

Picture Cards
Use the with "'Egg-ceptional' Letter F!" on page 64.

Tractor and Wagon Cards
Use with "A Crop of Letters" on page 66.

Farm Cards

Use with "Where's the Farmer?" on page 65.

Booklet Cover and Pages
Use with "A Funny Farm" on page 65.

Scarecrow Pattern
Use with "Patch 'em Up!" on page 66.

Name _____

Down on the Farm

✂ Cut.
Glue the pictures that begin with *F*.

Initial Sound /f/

B Is for Beach!

Beachcombing
Recognizing initial sound /b/

Beachcombing is a time-honored tradition that you can easily adapt to your classroom! Partially bury in your sand table small objects whose names begin with *B*. Also include objects whose names do not begin with *B*. Program two sand pails as shown and place a small sand shovel in each. Invite a pair of youngsters to use the shovels to carefully dig in the sand. When an object is found, the partners work together to decide whether its name begins with the /b/ sound. If it does, they place the item in the appropriate pail and then dig for another object. If it does not, they put the item in the other pail.

Beach Ball Bounce
Reciting the alphabet

Nothing says fun at the beach like playing with a big beach ball! Gather students and have each child hold the edge of a parachute and give it a good shake. Next, teach youngsters the chant below. At the end of the chant, begin to recite the alphabet with student help. Then toss a beach ball onto the parachute and encourage youngsters to bounce it around as long as possible while reciting letters. When the ball bounces off the parachute, start the game over at the beginning of the alphabet. Can your little ones keep the ball bouncing through all 26 letters?

Beach ball, beach ball,
Bounce it high; don't let it fall.
Up, down, all around,
These letters we will call:
A, B, C, D…

Shell Letters
Forming uppercase and lowercase B

Practicing the letter *B* is as easy as a day at the beach when you use pasta shells! In advance, program a sheet of construction paper with an uppercase *B*. Program a second sheet with a lowercase *B*. Laminate the sheets for durability if desired. Place the sheets and a supply of jumbo pasta shells in a center. Invite a child to select a sheet and use shells to form the letter on the sheet. Next, have him use more shells to form the letter beside the sheet. Encourage him to repeat the activity with the second sheet. If desired, have students return to the center for more practice with additional letters.

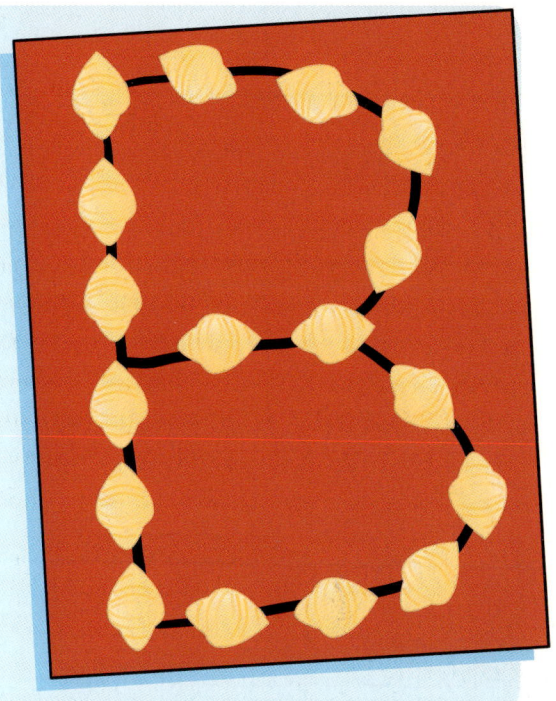

Beach Match
Matching uppercase and lowercase letters

Look what the tide brought in—lots and lots of letters! In advance, place a set of uppercase letter manipulatives in a clean sand pail. Also place a set of lowercase letter manipulatives in a different sand pail. Invite a pair of students to spread out the lowercase letters on a beach towel. Have one child choose an uppercase letter and identify it. Then have his partner find the matching lowercase letter. Encourage the twosome to discuss the pairing. If the students agree, they set the pair aside and switch roles. If they disagree, they work together to find the correct match before changing roles.

Letters in the Sand
Forming letters

Even if you're miles away from the shore, your little ones can enjoy writing on the beach! Just fill a shallow, lidded box with damp sand (or use your sand table). Demonstrate how to write a letter in the sand with your finger. Then invite a small group of students to take turns writing letters in the sand. If desired, provide an alphabet guide and encourage youngsters to write each letter. To erase the letters, simply smooth out the sand with the palm of your hand. Ready, set, write!

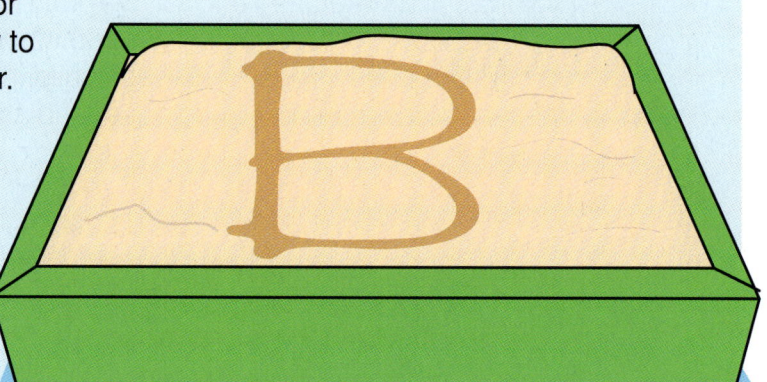

What Do You See at the Beach?
Using left-to-right progression

This adorable booklet is just the thing to encourage some beach reading! Give each child a copy of pages 78–80. Have her cut apart the booklet pages. Next, help her stack the pages in order behind the cover and staple the resulting booklet along the left-hand side. Read the booklet together; then have each child trace over the dashed letters to complete each sentence. On the last page, help her draw and write to complete the sentence. Invite her to color the pages as desired. What will your little ones see at the beach?

Sand and Sea Painting
Using descriptive language

Here's an activity that's sure to inspire plenty of adjective use! To prepare, mix play sand with yellow fingerpaint and place it in your art center. Also include water-thinned blue tempera paint and brushes. Give each child in this center a sheet of white construction paper and a spoonful of sand paint. Invite him to spread the sand along the bottom half of his paper. While he works, have him describe how the paint feels. Next, have him swirl the paintbrush in the watery blue paint and compare the texture with that of the sand paint. Then encourage him to paint the top half of his paper with the water paint and describe the differences between the two paints. When the paintings are dry, display them on a bulletin board and invite each child to say a word to describe the experience. Cool! Wet! Rough!

She Sells Seashells
Substituting beginning phonemes

Enjoy some wordplay with these silly seashore sounds! Write "She sells seashells by the seashore" on sentence strips and place the strips in a pocket chart. Also prepare one uppercase and three lowercase letter cards for each of the following consonants: *B, M, J,* and *T.* Read the sentence aloud. Help youngsters identify the beginning sound in each word. Next, show youngsters the *B* cards and say the sound the letter makes. Have students repeat the sound. Slip the four cards into the pocket chart, substituting the beginning letters as shown. Then reread the resulting silly sentence with student help. Use the remaining letter cards to continue substituting beginning letters and sounds in this same manner.

Booklet Cover and Page 1
Use with "What Do You See at the Beach?" on page 76.

What Do You See at the Beach?

Name _____

©The Mailbox® • Simply Seasonal ABCs • TEC60935

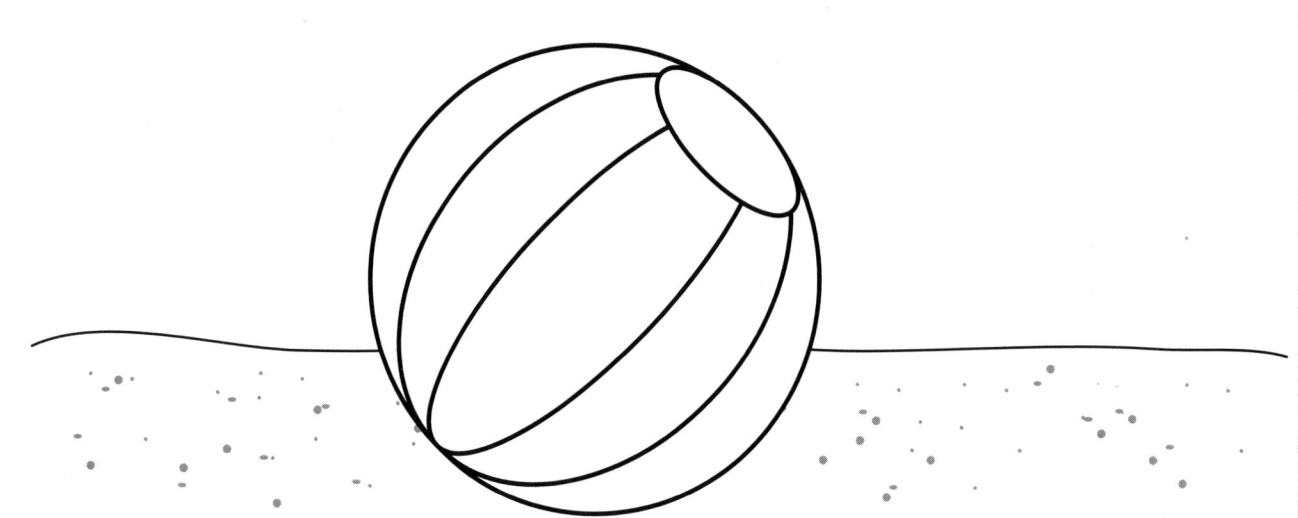

I see a ball.

Booklet Pages 2 and 3
Use with "What Do You See at the Beach?" on page 76.

Booklet Pages 4 and 5
Use with "What Do You See at the Beach?" on page 76.

I see a shell.

4

I see a _____.

5

Name _____ Matching Sounds

Beach Balls

🖍 Color the pictures whose names begin the same way.

✏️ Draw an X on the picture whose name is different.

©The Mailbox® • Simply Seasonal ABCs • TEC60935

Name _____ Rhyming Pictures

Shell Collectors

Color. Cut.

Glue to match the rhyming pictures.

©The Mailbox® • Simply Seasonal ABCs • TEC60935

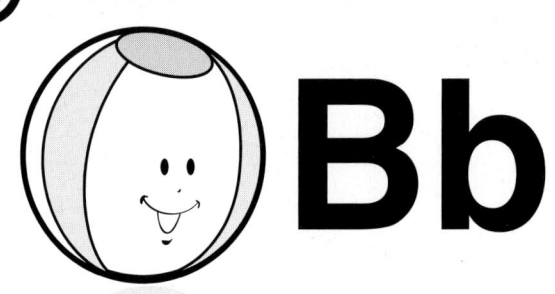

G Is for Garden!

Flower Garden
Identifying the sound /g/

Cultivate beginning sound knowledge as youngsters pull the weeds from this flower garden. Color and cut out a copy of the cards on page 88. Draw a flower on the back of each card that begins with the /g/ sound. Gather students in a circle and stack the cards picture side up in the middle of them. Also position a length of yarn in a circle to represent a garden. Then have one child at a time choose a card, name the picture, and tell whether the word begins with /g/ like *garden.* Help her check her answer by looking for a flower on the back of the card. Have her place the card in the garden if the picture begins with /g/. If it does not, she places the card in a weed pile outside of the garden.

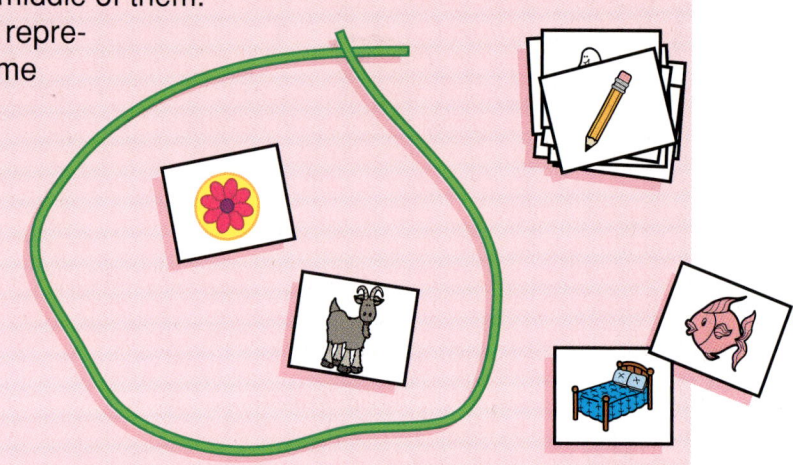

Grow, Grow, Grow
Identifying letters

Watch youngsters' letter skills grow with this partner game. Color and cut out two copies of the flower cards on page 87. If desired, laminate the cards. Also create a set of alphabet cards that includes at least five extra cards with the uppercase and lowercase letter *G*. To play, a pair of students lays the flower cards and alphabet cards facedown in two separate stacks. Each child, in turn, draws an alphabet card and names the letter. If it is a *G,* he turns over one flower card and says, "Grow, grow, grow!" Then he places the alphabet card in a discard pile. Play continues in the same manner until one child has turned over all three cards to show a fully grown flower.

Paired Veggies
Matching uppercase and lowercase letters

Sell youngsters on letter-matching skills with a stop at this vegetable stand. Color and cut out a copy of the vegetable patterns on page 89. Program each vegetable with the corresponding lowercase beginning letter as shown. Also gather a set of uppercase magnetic letters and place them in a basket. Attach the vegetables to a magnetic board. If desired, use a dry-erase marker to draw on the board a vegetable stand similar to the one shown. Invite a student to choose a magnetic letter, say its name, and then decide whether it can be paired with a featured lowercase letter. If it does match, he attaches it to the corresponding vegetable. Have the child repeat the process until all the vegetables have been matched.

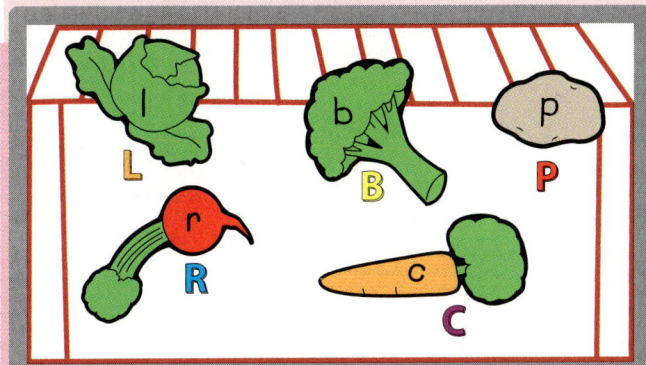

Veggie Riddles
Identifying letter-sound relationships

Your little ones will eat up these riddles! Read a set of clues to youngsters and have them repeat the featured letter and say its sound. Then help them solve the riddle. Continue in the same manner for each riddle. If desired, have youngsters help create other veggie riddles.

This veggie is green.
It grows above the ground.
It looks like a little tree.
Its name begins with *B*.

This veggie is orange.
It grows below the ground.
Rabbits love to eat it.
Its name begins with *C*.

This veggie is brown.
It grows below the ground.
French fries are made from it.
Its name begins with *P*.

Gardening Tune
Generating rhyming words

Picking veggies from this garden gives youngsters plenty of rhyming practice. In advance, make several colored construction paper copies of the vegetable patterns on page 89. Laminate and cut out the vegetables. Use a dry-erase marker to write a CVC word—such as *cat, man,* or *bug*—on each vegetable. Have youngsters sit in a circle; then spread the vegetables in the middle of them. Sing the song below to students and then have one child choose a vegetable. Help her read the word on the vegetable and then name a corresponding rhyming word. Repeat the activity several times, asking a different child to choose a vegetable each time.

(sung to the tune of "On Top of Old Smokey")

In the farmer's garden, he works hard all day
To grow fruits and veggies, so healthy we'll stay.
Let's help him pick veggies; I think that it's time.
Pull one from the garden and then make a rhyme.

Go, Gopher!
Demonstrating an understanding of positional words

This little gopher helps youngsters practice positional words as they create a cute booklet. Give each child a copy of pages 90 and 91 and have him color the pages and patterns. After reading the text on each booklet page aloud, help him cut out the patterns. Guide him to glue the door pattern in the space provided. Then help him cut out the booklet pages, sequence them, and staple them together along the left-hand side. Tape a length of yarn onto the back of the gopher pattern and then tape the other end onto the back of the booklet. Help each child read his booklet as he manipulates the gopher to illustrate each positional word.

Garden Goodies
Identifying letter-sound relationships

What grows in a garden? Your little gardeners will have many ideas during this beginning sound activity. Place a set of alphabet cards in a watering can or plastic pail. Invite youngsters to sit in a circle and discuss things that can be found in a garden, such as flowers, insects, tools, seeds, and vegetables. Next, pass the watering can to a child. Have him draw a card, read the letter, and name an object whose name begins with the letter. Then have him pass the can to another child and continue in the same manner until each child has had a turn.

Flower Cards
Use with "Grow, Grow, Grow" on page 84.

©The Mailbox® • Simply Seasonal ABCs • TEC60935

Picture Cards
Use with "Flower Garden" on page 84.

Vegetable Patterns
Use with "Paired Veggies" on page 85 and "Gardening Tune" on page 86.

Booklet Cover and Pages 1–3
Use with "Go, Gopher!" on page 86.

name

©The Mailbox® • Simply Seasonal ABCs • TEC60935

Go under the sun.

1

Go beside the tools.

2

Go in front of the scarecrow.

3

Booklet Pages 4–5 and Patterns
Use with "Go, Gopher!" on page 86.

Go between the fences.

4

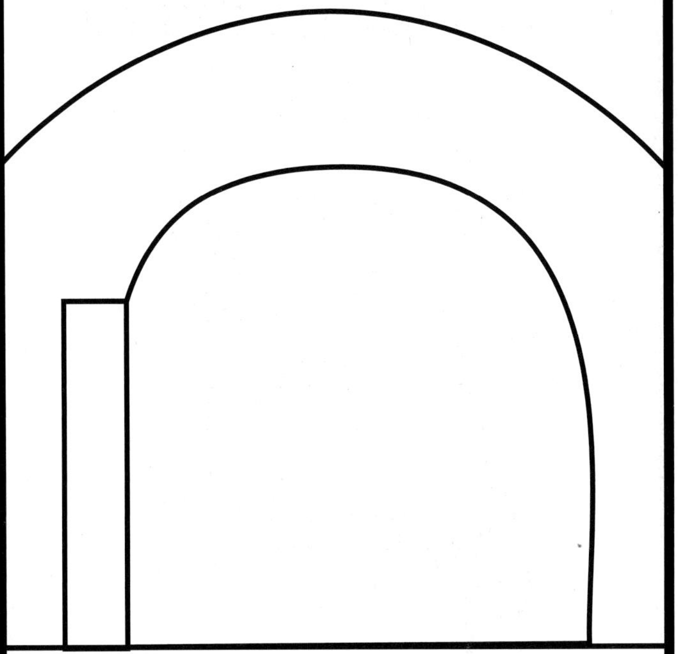

Go in your home!

5

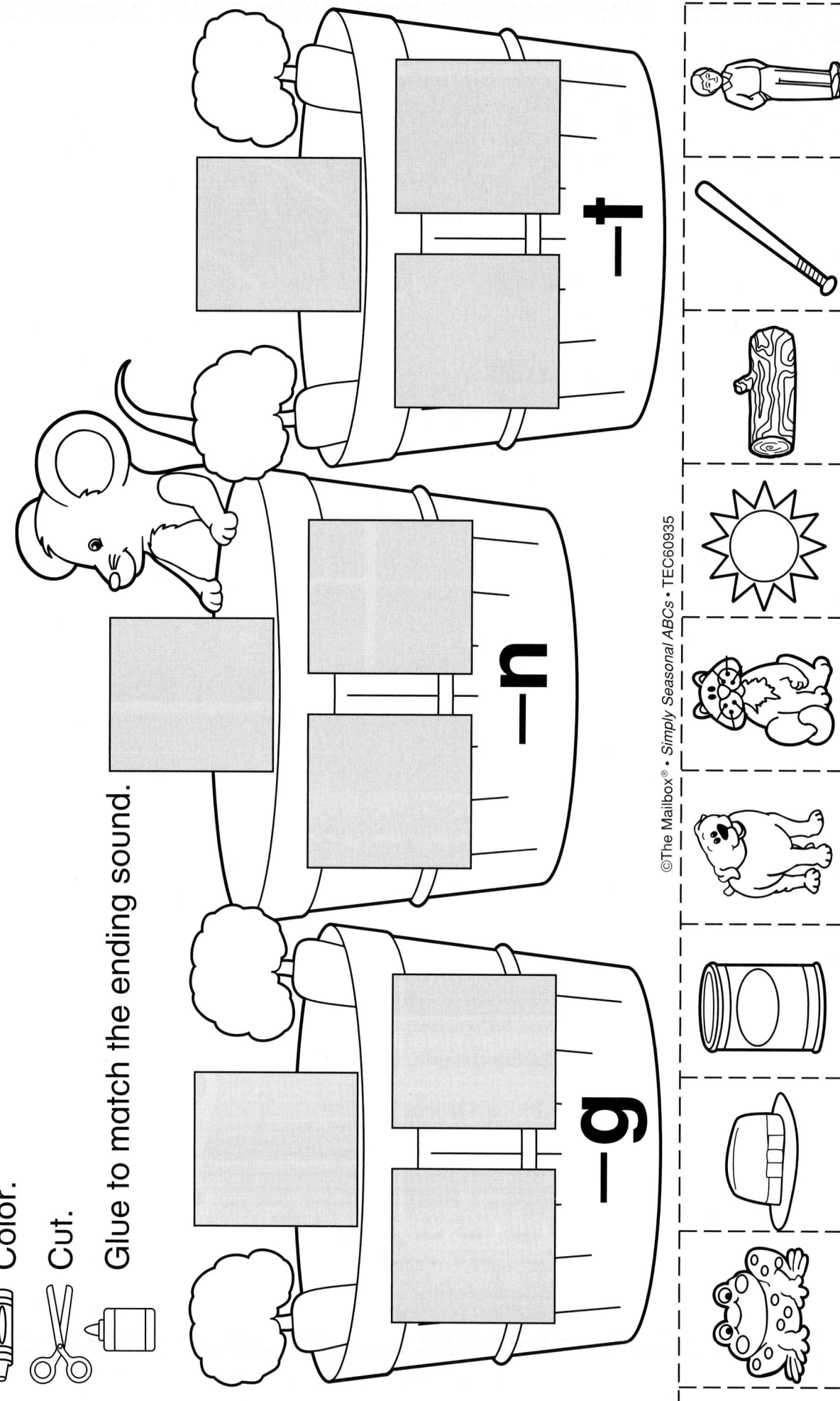

Gg

S Is for Sunflower!

Sunflower Seed Ss
Forming the letter S

Watch your little ones' letter formation skills bloom with this sunny activity! For each child, program the center of a small yellow paper plate with a large letter *S*. Next, cut slits in the rim of each plate to resemble sunflower petals. Fold up every other petal to complete the look. Give each child in a small group a prepared sunflower and access to a washable black stamp pad. Have each child trace over the letter *S* on her sunflower and then press fingerprints over the letter to represent sunflower seeds. Mount the completed sunflowers on a wall or bulletin board for a sunny display.

Sunflower Match
Matching uppercase and lowercase letters

Pick this center idea for reinforcing letter awareness! To prepare, copy the sunflower patterns (page 98) onto yellow construction paper to make 26 flowers. Cut out the flowers and program each with a different uppercase letter. Tape a craft stick to the back of each flower to resemble a stem. Next, program each of 26 small plain paper cups (flowerpots) with a different lowercase letter. Stick play dough or clay in each cup. Store the flowerpots and sunflowers at a center. To use, two students take turns "planting" each sunflower in its corresponding flowerpot. For an added challenge, have the pair identify each letter pair and then place the matched letter pairs in alphabetical order.

The Seed Grew!
Reinforcing concepts of print

You're in for a bumper crop of print concepts when youngsters make these sunny little booklets! Make a class supply of the booklet cover and pages on pages 98–100. Give each child in a small group a set of copies and have her cut out the booklet cover and pages. Help her stack the pages in order behind the cover and staple the booklet along the left-hand side. Then read the booklet with the group. Have a volunteer show you where to begin reading on each page and where to stop. Invite another volunteer to indicate when to turn the pages. You may also wish to have volunteers point out letters, punctuation marks, capital letters, and words. Next, invite each child to color the pages. Encourage each child to read the booklet back to you and then take it home to share with her family.

Sunflower Snacks
Following oral directions

Youngsters are sure to follow your directions when a scrumptious sunflower snack is the result! Purchase a class supply of round crackers, spreadable pineapple-flavored cream cheese, and cheese slices. Give each child a cracker on a napkin. Explain to students that they are going to follow your directions to make a sunflower snack. Then ask each child to use a plastic knife to spread cream cheese on her cracker. Next, give her a cheese slice and tell her to cut it into small triangles. Instruct her to place the triangles around the cracker to resemble sunflower petals. Then invite her to enjoy her snack. Yum!

See It Grow
Connecting to literature

After a reading of Eve Bunting's classic tale *Sunflower House,* enjoy this craft activity with your youngsters. Then use the results to make a long-lasting sunflower house that's just right for some cozy reading. Give each child a large paper plate and have him sponge-paint it brown. When the paint is dry, have him tear two sheets of yellow construction paper into petals. Instruct him to glue the petals to the back of the plate, overlapping them to fully surround it. Next, have him fold up every other petal to fluff up the flower. To make the sunflower house, cut off the top and bottom flaps of a large appliance box; then cut a door in one side. Paint the sides green and allow the paint to dry. Invite each child to recall the sunflowers growing in the story and then tape his sunflower to the house. Add stems and leaves from dark green construction paper as desired. Complete the house with a couple of soft pillows and a copy of *Sunflower House.* Then invite pairs of youngsters to curl up in the house and enjoy the book together.

Sounds Like *Sun!*
Naming words that begin with /s/

Display a beautiful bouquet of /s/ sound words! To prepare, make several yellow construction paper copies of the sunflower patterns on page 98. Cut out the sunflowers and store them in your circle area. Gather your students and explain that you need their help to think of lots of words that begin with the same sound as *sunflower.* Then invite volunteers to say /s/ words while you record each on a different sunflower cutout. When a desired number of words has been recorded, reread all the words with student help. Then mount the sunflowers with stems above a construction paper vase cutout.

Big Yellow Sunflowers
Using descriptive language

Hmm—how would your students describe sunflowers? Find out with this simple circle-time activity! Pass a real sunflower around the circle and encourage each youngster to examine it carefully. Then invite each child, in turn, to complete the sentence "The sunflower is..." If desired, prompt students to use their senses of smell, touch, and sight to help generate a variety of words. You're sure to get plenty of descriptive words in a short amount of time!

Did You Ever See...
Substituting beginning sounds

Watch your youngsters' smiles bloom with each verse of this silly song! Using magnetic letters, spell the word *sunflower* on a cookie sheet. Also have on hand a variety of consonant magnetic letters. Gather your little ones and teach them the song below. As you sing the word *sunflower*, point to the word on the cookie sheet. Then replace the *S* in *sunflower* with a different consonant and say the resulting word. During the next repetition of the song, sing the silly word in place of *sunflower*. Repeat this process several times for guaranteed fun!

(sung to the tune of
"Did You Ever See a Lassie?")

Did you ever see a sunflower,
A sunflower, a sunflower?
Did you ever see a sunflower?
It starts with /s/!

Sunflower Patterns
Use with "Sunflower Match" on page 94 and "Sounds Like *Sun*!" on page 96.

Booklet Cover
Use with "The Seed Grew!" on page 95.

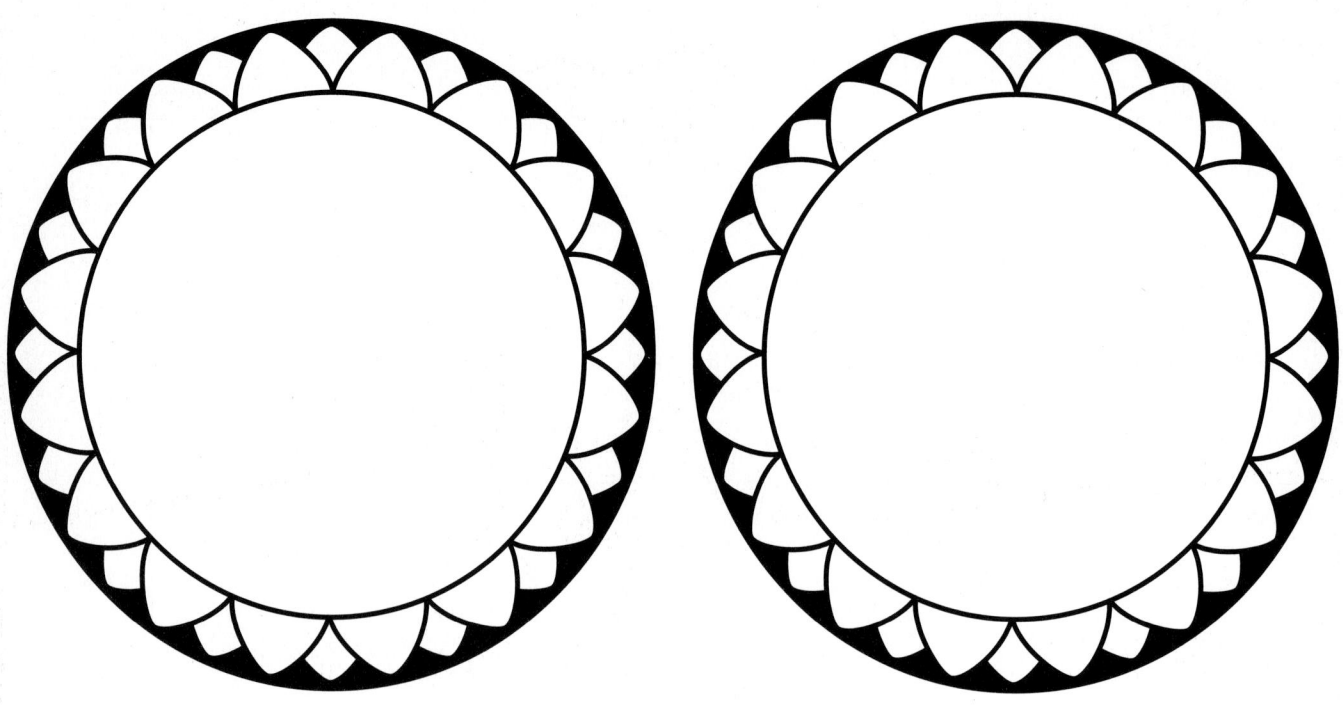

The Seed Grew!

Name _____

©The Mailbox® • Simply Seasonal ABCs • TEC60935

Booklet Pages 3 and 4
Use with "The Seed Grew!" on page 95.

The plant grew and grew.

3

And now it's taller than me!

4

Name _____   Initial consonant S

Sunflower Sounds

 Cut.  Glue the pictures that start with *S*.

©The Mailbox® • *Simply Seasonal ABCs* • TEC60935

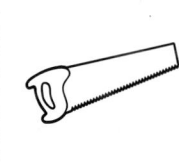     

Sunny Sunflowers

Color the sunflowers with matching letters.

Ss

W Is for Watermelon!

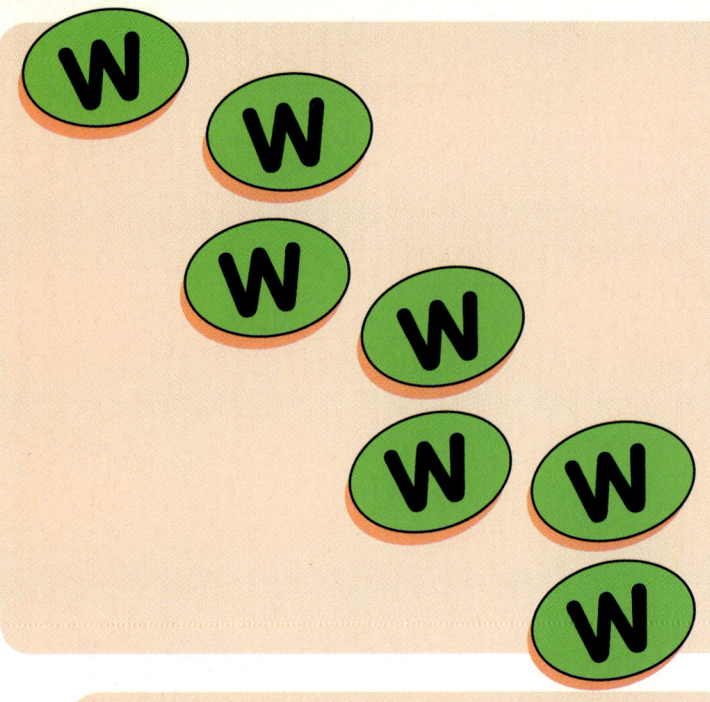

A Watermelon Walk
Associating W with /w/

Little ones are sure to remember the sound of the letter *W* when they go for a stroll through this watermelon patch! Make a supply of large watermelon cutouts. Label each one with the letter *W*. Then use Con-Tact paper to adhere them to the floor to make a path. Encourage each child to walk or hop along the watermelon path, saying /w/ each time he lands on a watermelon.

From Seed to Watermelon
Sequencing pictures

Cultivate youngsters' sequencing skills with a toe-tapping song! Color a copy of the sequencing cards (page 108) and cut them out. Then prepare the cards for flannelboard use. Place the first card on the flannelboard. Then lead youngsters in singing the song shown. Sing the song five more times, creating a new verse from each line in the provided sequence and placing each corresponding card on the flannelboard.

(sung to the tune of "He's Got the Whole World in His Hands")

You plant a small seed in the ground.
You plant a small seed in the ground.
You plant a small seed in the ground.
You plant a small seed in the ground.

A tiny vine grows from the seed.
The leaves are growing on the vine.
Among the leaves, the flowers bloom.
The watermelon starts to grow.
It's time to eat this juicy treat!

 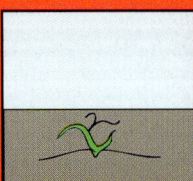    

A Lovely Sight
Recognizing the letter W

Get ready to see big smiles when your little ones perform this action rhyme! Write the rhyme below on chart paper and post it in your large-group area. Invite youngsters to find and circle each *W* in the rhyme. When students are comfortable reciting the rhyme, encourage them to add the provided actions.

Watermelon, you are very small.
It seems you're hardly there at all.

Use fingers to show a small watermelon.

Watermelon, you begin to grow.
But you are growing oh so slow.

Use arms to show a medium-size watermelon.

Watermelon, you're a lovely sight.
I think I'll take a nice big bite!
Crunch!

Use arms to show a huge watermelon.

Pretend to take a big bite out of the watermelon.

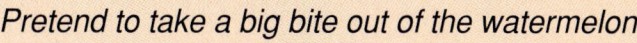

Lots of Leaves
Naming words that begin with /w/

This leafy activity results in a display that's simply divine! Tape a length of thick green yarn to a watermelon cutout to resemble a vine. Label the watermelon with an uppercase and a lowercase *W*. Then display the watermelon and vine at student level on a wall in your classroom. Give each youngster a green leaf cutout. Have her write (or dictate as you write) a word that begins with /w/ on the cutout. After each child tapes her cutout to the vine, invite her to read her word.

A Pleasing Picnic
Matching uppercase and lowercase letters

Any way you slice it, this puzzle center is just plain fun! Make several construction paper copies of the watermelon pattern on page 109. Cut out the patterns. Label the boxes on each cutout with corresponding uppercase and lowercase letters. Then cut each watermelon slice in half, using a different puzzle cut each time. Store the cutouts in a picnic basket and place the basket on a blanket in a center. Then invite a pair of youngsters to the picnic area and encourage them to remove the watermelon slices and match the halves to show corresponding uppercase and lowercase letters.

Where the Watermelon Grows!
Naming words that rhyme

Youngsters sing the traditional song "Down by the Bay" and make up new verses to place in this class book! For each child, program a 12" x 18" sheet of paper with the prompt shown. Lead youngsters in singing the song "Down by the Bay." Give each child a sheet of prepared paper and help her complete the sentence with two rhyming words. Encourage her to illustrate her writing. Then stack the completed pages together with a cover titled "Down by the Bay." Sing the song with youngsters several times, using each page in the book to make a new verse.

Did you ever see a <u>cat</u> with a flowered <u>hat</u> down by the bay?

So Many Seeds
Identifying final consonants

Your youngsters won't find any seedless watermelons in this phonics center! Make two large construction paper watermelon slices. Label one slice with the letter *T* and the second slice with the letter *N*. Cut out a copy of the picture cards on page 109 and glue each one to a black construction paper seed cutout. Place the melons and seeds at a center. A youngster chooses a seed and says the name of the picture. He identifies the final sound in the word and then places the seed on the corresponding slice. He continues in the same way for each remaining seed.

Wonderful Watermelon
Identifying the high-frequency word *it*

Here's a cute little booklet that will help youngsters remember the high-frequency word *it*! Make a copy of the booklet pages on page 110 for each child. Encourage each youngster to color the pictures as desired and then cut out the pages. Have her glue the pages, in order, to a 6" x 18" strip of red construction paper, accordion-folded as shown. Help her glue the folded strip between two green construction paper covers. Then prompt her to write the title shown and her name on the front cover. Help each student read her booklet, encouraging her to point to the word *it* on each page. Then invite her to take her booklet home to share with her family.

Wonderful Watermelon by Lauren

Grow it. | Pick it. | Slice it. | Eat it. Yum!

Sequencing Cards
Use with "From Seed to Watermelon" on page 104.

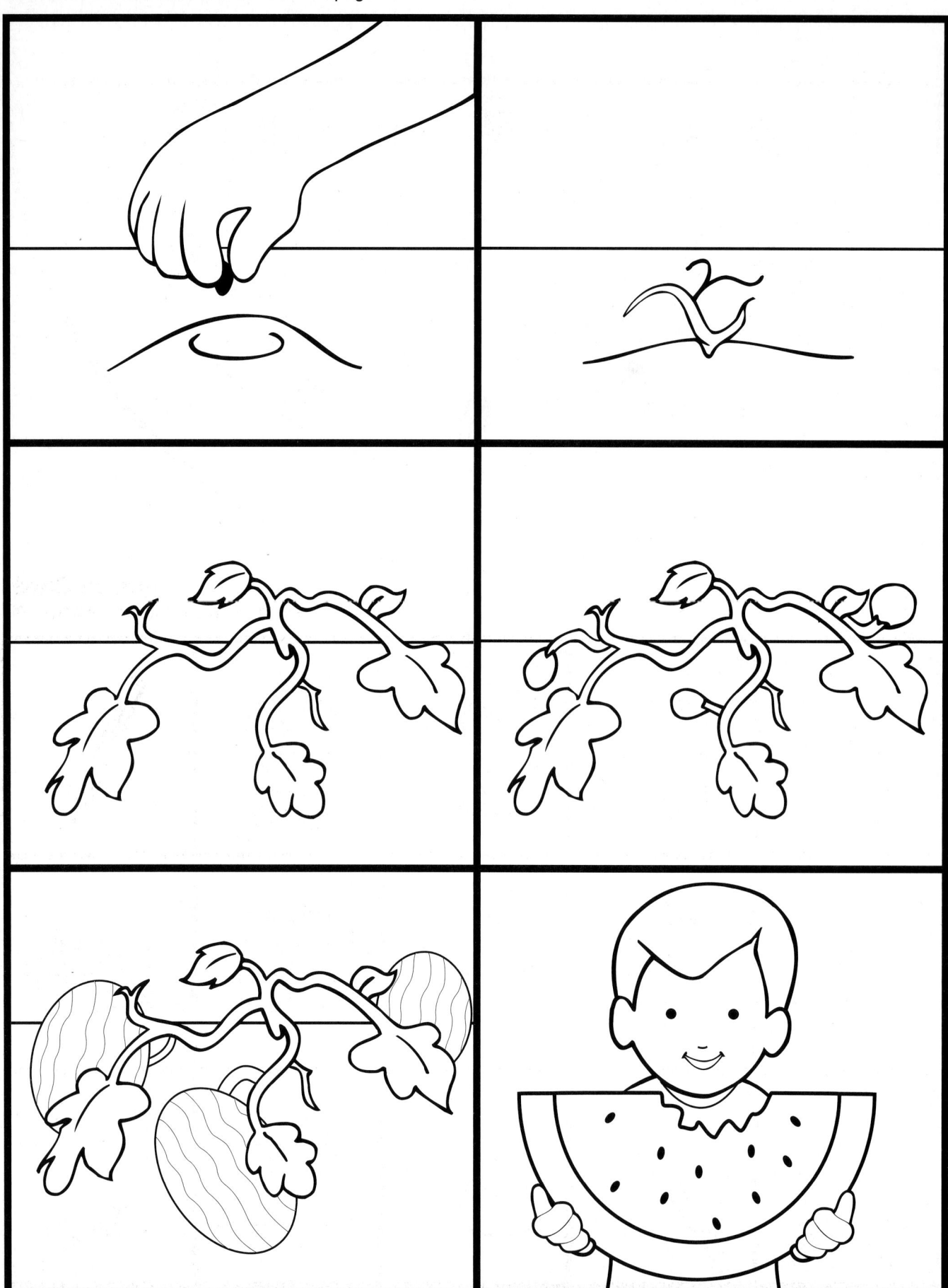

Watermelon Pattern
Use with "A Pleasing Picnic" on page 106.

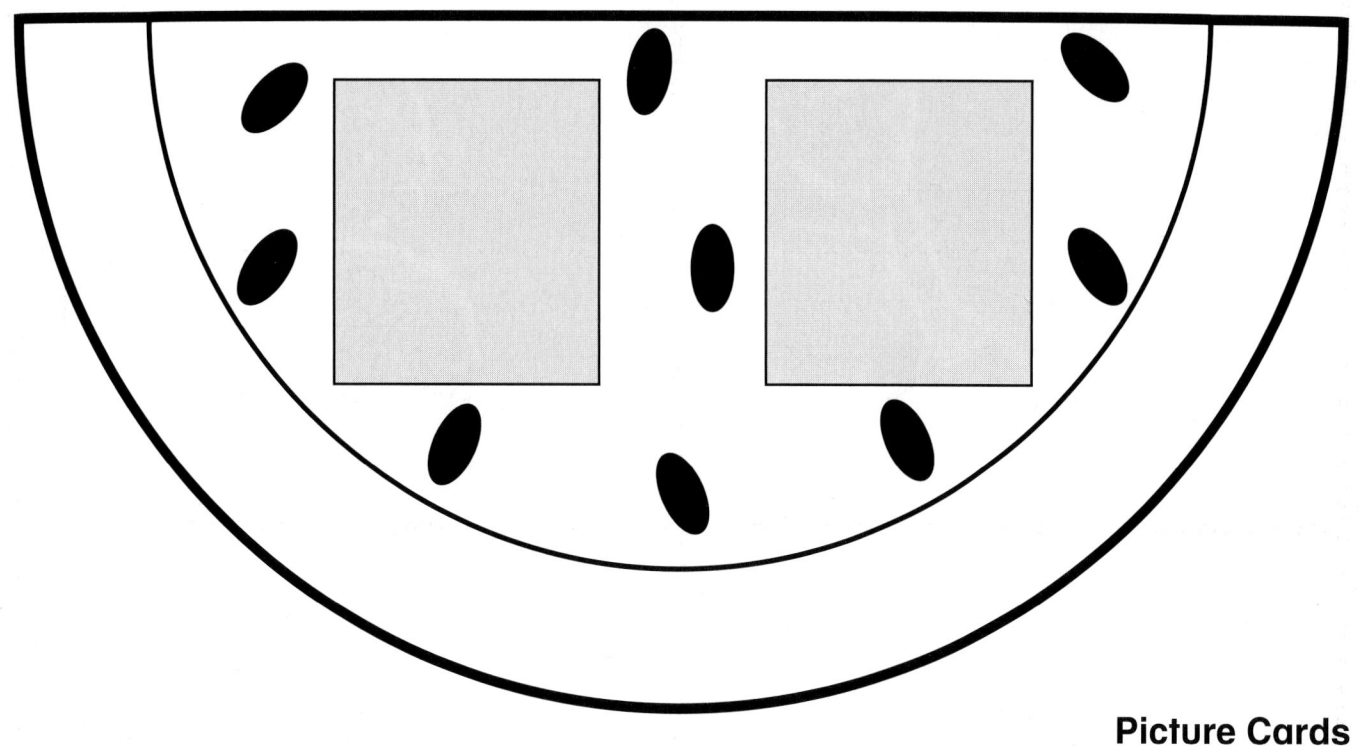

Picture Cards
Use with "So Many Seeds" on page 107.

©The Mailbox® • *Simply Seasonal ABCs* • TEC60935

Booklet Pages
Use with "Wonderful Watermelon" on page 107.

Name _____

Sorting by Word Family

Tasty Watermelon!

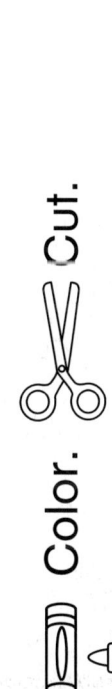 Color. ✂ Cut.

Glue each watermelon to the matching word family.

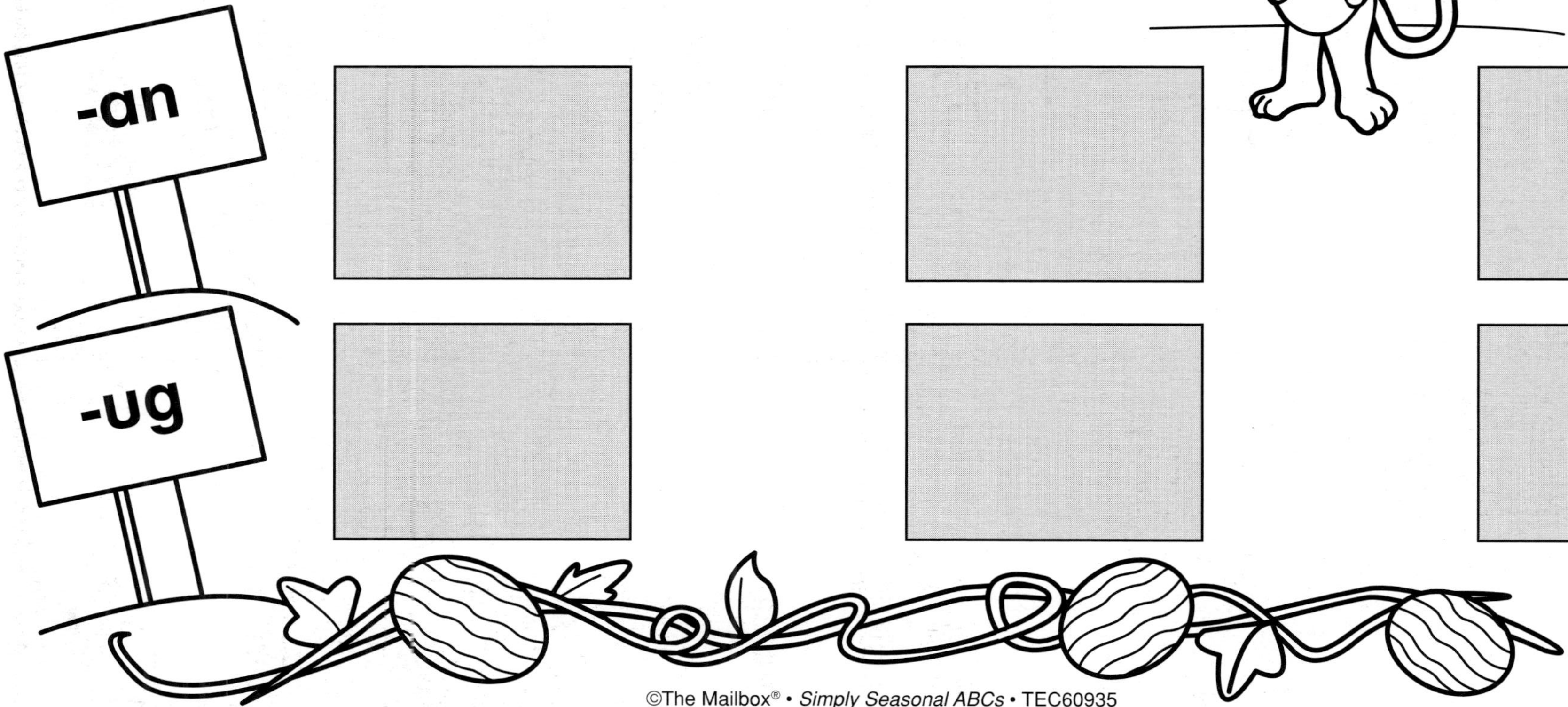

-an

-ug

Ww